Online death threats are depressingly common. But how do you separate them into those issued by sheer fantasists, and those coming from someone with genuinely deadly intent? In *Personal Threat Management: The Practitioner's Guide to Keeping Clients Safer*, Philip Grindell explains how to spot the difference – and what to do when you realize someone really does pose a threat. Timely and valuable to anyone in the public eye.

Richard Madeley, writer and broadcaster

This book will be a valuable resource for individuals beginning in Behaviour Threat Assessment (BTA) or those who have been practising for years. Based on his years of experience in successfully assessing and managing numerous cases, Philip has put together best practice examples in an informative and understandable manner. I would recommend this book to Law Enforcement, Mental Health, Security Professionals, Attorneys, Human Resource Professionals, and anyone who is currently working on a BTA team or those putting a team together.

William J. Zimmerman, Detective U.S. Capitol Police – Threat Assessment Section (Retired)

Philip is an unusual combination of an academic and operational expert, and anyone interested in protecting themselves or others should read this book.

Neil Basu QPM, former head of UK Counter Terrorism Policing

Abuse, intimidation and threats are sad facts of life in the modern world. How should you respond to them? Should you be worried about escalation to physical harm? How should you protect your clients and their families or co-workers? Philip Grindell discusses how the process of behavioural threat assessment can help to answer these and related questions. The perspective he offers is highly practical, based on decades of field experience. If you want to prevent people from becoming victims of violence, put this book on your reading list.

Dr Stephen D. Hart, PhD, Director and Threat Assessment Specialist, President, Canadian Association of Threat Assessment Professionals

For those advising individuals and organizations on threat risks, it's essential to understand who and what one is dealing with. Grindell's decades of real-world experience mean his voice is ignored at your and (more importantly) your client's peril.

Julian Pike, Lawyer and Head of Reputation Management and Sport at Farrer & Co

Philip Grindell brings 30 years as a police officer matched with years in threat assessment and management to bear in a book that everyone involved in the protection of public figures should get their hands on. Practical, rather than academic, Philip's work covers a number of well-known case studies involving public figures, from angles previously not looked at. I believe that I would have benefited from such insights in the time that I served and protected the most famous person in the world.

Rory Steyn, formerly Team Leader of President Nelson Mandela's Personal Protection Team. Co-Founder, NSA Global Security Consultants

If you are serious about security, you will find some great insights in *Personal Threat Management: The Practitioner's Guide to Keeping Clients Safer*. Phil Grindell's professional experience and practical, real-world strategies are evident in every chapter, offering clear, actionable advice for tackling modern security challenges. Whether you're dealing with physical security, online threats or crisis management, this book is a comprehensive and useful guide to keeping people and assets safe.

G.B. Jones, Chief Safety and Security Officer,
FIFA World Cup 2026; former FBI Special Agent

Philip Grindell is one of the few threat assessment experts in the world with extensive experience advising public figures, politicians and royal families. In *The Practitioner's Guide to Keeping Clients Safer*, Grindell educates on the science of threat assessment and the nuanced art of managing victim fear. His compassionate view of ensuring clients feel safer demonstrates why his expertise is in demand. This is a book for threat assessment practitioners by a true practitioner.

Gabrielle Thompson, Threat Assessment
Expert and Consultant to public figures and corporations

Informed by the author's professional experiences and illustrated with dozens of real-life case studies, *Personal Threat Management* provides its readers with a solid introduction to today's threat management principles and practices. The book is easily read and readily understandable as Grindell explains basic concepts and practical approaches to keeping individuals safe. *Personal Threat Management* is essential reading for anyone seeking to distinguish between those who make a threat and those who pose a threat.

Frederick S. Calhoun, author
Effective Threat Management: A Primer

I highly recommend *Personal Threat Management: The Practitioner's Guide to Keeping Clients Safer* for anyone interested in threat management. Grindell is a real security expert and practitioner who writes clearly and intelligently, which allows for immediate comprehension of complex concepts. Well done, Philip!

James Hamilton, former FBI Special Agent and Recognized Personal Security Expert

I met Philip Grindell in February 2019 after he had set up the team in [the UK] Parliament after the murder of my sister Jo in June 2016. Philip has been a huge help in advising both The Jo Cox Foundation and me personally on any concerns regarding safety and security. He is one of the world's leading advisers on personal threat risks and this book is a significant resource to anyone involved in helping others feel safer.

Kim Leadbeater, Member of Parliament for Spen Valley (sister of Jo Cox MP)

If you want to know about Personal Threat Management, then there is no one else to read but Phillip Grindell! Phillip seamlessly integrates his vast experience, gravitas and knowledge to provide a powerful read from which all security professionals can gain vital knowledge and understanding. Thoughtfully, humbly and practically, the author takes us on a journey through the intricacies of understanding threat and risk so we can start to develop our senses to manage different situations where we could be vulnerable. This book would have been invaluable to me 30 years ago when I began my security career, and I regularly turn to Phillip for subject matter advice. I'm very proud to see him commit his wise thoughts and expertise to paper. I can recommend this book as there is simply no other on the market that in my opinion contains the academic refinement and practical advice this does on the subject. Understanding and recognizing is everything; the security sector will provide a better service to our clients because of this book!

Guy Batchelor MBA, CTRM, MSyl, VR Director, Minerva Elite Ltd, Former UK Special Mission Force Soldier and Officer

Personal Threat Management is a great primer for those new to threat assessment, written in a very accessible style and packed with immediately useful information. Security expert Philip Grindell nicely clarifies often misunderstood key terms and concepts, illustrating them with numerous case examples and illuminating important nuances in decision-making. His text reflects his many years of field experience combined with a firm grasp of contemporary research on the assessment of threats, offering a clear standard of professionalism for those facing the many challenges in our expanding global landscape of risks. I applaud his sensitivity to clients' fear but with his emphasis that the primary avenue for reducing concerns is through sound threat assessment and management practice. This book is particularly useful in meeting the needs of practitioners in the UK and other European countries, where cultural, legal and organizational factors will differ from those in the USA. Grindell's style is refreshingly personal, as though the reader is sitting down with him and just listening to his many nuggets of wisdom and guidance.

Stephen White, PhD Threat assessment expert and author, and former president of Work Trauma Services, Inc.

In this timely work, the author delivers a master class in threat assessment, management and personal safety. Drawing from a wealth of experience in law enforcement and security, the book offers invaluable insights into the minds of fixated individuals and the escalation of threatening behaviour. What sets this book apart is its comprehensive approach, blending historical examples with contemporary cases to illustrate the evolving nature of threats. The author's emphasis on 'intuition' as a critical safety tool is compelling, providing readers with practical strategies to enhance their situational awareness. From dissecting pathways of escalating threats to exploring the nuances of high-stakes situations, this book equips security professionals, business leaders and potential targets with the knowledge to identify, assess and manage potential dangers effectively. This is not just a book; it's an essential guide for navigating the complex landscape of personal and professional security in our modern world. It is a must-read for anyone serious about threat assessment, management, and personal safety.

Dr Lorraine Sheridan, PhD Forensic Psychologist, Adjunct Associate Professor in Psychology, *author Psycho-Criminological Approaches to Stalking Behaviour: An International Perspective*

Philip first became active in my protection following a series of newspaper stories which led to extensive hostility and threats on social media and internationally. When something like this happens, you feel vulnerable at every level. Philip has spent decades helping others like me feel safer, and this book reflects that wealth of experience and expertise. While written for security professionals, it is equally useful for public figures operating in an increasingly hostile environment. I look forward to adding it to my library and encouraging others in Parliament to read it.

Sarah Champion, Member of Parliament for Rotherham and the first female Chair of the International Development Select Committee

Personal Threat Management: The Practitioner's Guide to Keeping Clients Safer is an essential and timely resource for professionals in the field of security and safety. Written by a seasoned expert with deep operational experience, this guide offers a comprehensive and practical framework for understanding and mitigating threats faced by high-profile clients. From political figures to business leaders and celebrities, Grindell's insights demystify the complex world of personal safety and protective intelligence. The book is structured to provide both theoretical understanding and actionable strategies. Part 1 explores various threats, ranging from communicated threats and unwanted attention to the more severe risks of workplace violence and fixated threats. Through real-life case studies, Grindell illustrates how these dangers manifest and offer readers invaluable advice on assessing the level of risk, identifying behavioral indicators, and responding effectively. Part 2 shifts focus to practical threat management, giving readers the tools needed to gather intelligence, remain situationally aware, and handle escalating threats. Not only does Grindell emphasize the importance of trusting one's intuition, but also he stresses the critical need to avoid complacency, particularly in high-stakes environments. His use of actual client experiences, though anonymized, adds real-world gravitas to the text, allowing readers to visualize how these scenarios play out in practice. This book is more than just a reference; it is a guide to proactive threat management. Grindell's insights into the psychology behind fixated behaviours, the role of social media in facilitating unwanted attention, and the fine line between security and safety are indispensable for professionals. *Personal Threat Management* is an essential read for anyone charged with protecting individuals in an increasingly complex world. It will empower its readers to not only safeguard their clients but to ensure they feel safer in the process.

Totti Karpela, CTM, CETAP, Threat Assessment Specialist and former police officer, National Police of Finland

Personal Threat Management

The practitioner's guide
to keeping clients safer

PHILIP
GRINDELL

First published in Great Britain by Practical Inspiration Publishing, 2025

© Philip Grindell, 2025

The moral rights of the author have been asserted.

ISBN   978-17-88606-52-3 (hardback)
          978-17-88606-53-0 (paperback)
          978-17-88606-55-4 (epub)
          978-17-88606-54-7 (Kindle)

Want to bulk-buy copies of this book for your team and colleagues? We can customize the content and co-brand Personal Threat Management to suit your business's needs.

Please email info@practicalinspiration.com for more details.

Practical Inspiration
Publishing

For my wife, Amanda, for believing in me.

Contents

Foreword...xv

Prologue.. xvii

Part 1: Understanding the threats............................ 1

Chapter 1: Security vs safety 3

Chapter 2: Fixated threats 19

Chapter 3: Unwanted attention 29

Chapter 4: Communicated threats... 39

Chapter 5: Work-related violence... 55

Chapter 6: Threat escalation... 69

Chapter 7: Pre-attack warning behaviours............................ 77

Chapter 8: Safer events and functions 95

Part 2: Managing the threats............................... 109

Chapter 9: Interviewing and gathering information 111

Chapter 10: Be situationally aware....................................... 119

Chapter 11: Trust your intuition 127

Chapter 12: Personal safety... 133

Chapter 13: Stop giving away your secrets........................... 139

Chapter 14: Complacency kills... 149

Chapter 15: The security profession..................................... 155

Afterword 165

Endnotes and further publications 169

The author 181

Index 183

Foreword

*P*ersonal *Threat Management: The Practitioner's Guide to Keeping Clients Safer* is a thoughtful, pragmatic, useful book. Philip Grindell, a retired Metropolitan Police Officer and now leader of an important private sector security consultancy, deftly pulls together research from behavioural threat assessment and management, and related areas of security planning and operations. The author utilizes his 30+ years of law enforcement and security expertise and experience to lead the reader on a detailed and commonsense journey to better physical, psychological and reputational safety.

Personal Threat Management is divided into two sections: (1) Understanding the Threats; and (2) Managing the Threats. In each section Philip Grindell provides concrete examples, cases and anecdotes that illustrate major themes and points. His chapters are filled with trenchant observations and helpful (and sometimes potentially life-saving) advice.

Grindell writes in a clear and inviting style. His comprehensive knowledge of these subjects, and his caring about persons who might find themselves in harm's way, are powerfully apparent.

This excellent book will be of interest and use to public officials and officers who want to learn more about preventing targeted violence, to security professionals and practitioners, to corporate, educational and industry leaders, and to members of the public.

Philip Grindell's readable book is, in my view, very likely to prevent harm, and perhaps even to save lives.

Robert A. Fein, Ph.D., ABP, Forensic and National Security Psychologist and the co-author of *Preventing Assassination: US Secret Service Exceptional Case Study Project*

Prologue

In 2016, I was a Detective Inspector in the Metropolitan Police Specialist Operations Command when, following the assassination of a British Labour politician called Jo Cox, Neil Basu, the UK head of Counter Terrorism Policing asked me to set up and run a team dedicated to stopping the next attack on a Member of Parliament. (The case of Jo Cox MP is covered in more detail in Chapter 2, and endnotes 4, 20 and 21.)

I recall sitting in my office in the Houses of Parliament, faced with the challenges set for me, unclear how to achieve them. I spoke with the Senior Investigating Officer from the Jo Cox investigation to ask whether he could share anything to help me prevent the next attack. He couldn't.

The challenge was that despite a huge protective security operation, with every Member of Parliament having access to a carefully thought-out set of security measures, most MPs still felt unsafe. More 'stuff' wasn't making them feel safer.

By coincidence, my new role in Parliament coincided with my studying for an MSc in Security Management as a mature student. As I progressed in my studies, my research, passion and operational application caused me to focus my dissertation on those who target public figures. The title was 'Targeted Violence Towards British Political Figures – Where Should the Security Manager Focus?'.

One of the key research projects that was of particular interest was initiated to provide operational expertise for the US Secret Service who were tasked with protecting the US President, among others. This research was titled 'Preventing Assassination: Secret Service Exceptional Case Study Project'.[1] During a trip to Harvard University, I had the good fortune to meet with one of the authors, Dr Robert Fein, where I spoke at a conference on global threats to female politicians. Dr Fein then introduced me to other scholars and experts in Protective Intelligence, who shared their expertise with me. I'm indebted to them for their generosity and wisdom.

These introductions ignited my passion, which motivated me to conduct extensive research and apply what I had learned in practice, which continues today.

In 2017, I was handed a piece of paper with six lines on it. Because of the expertise I'd acquired, I was able to identify that this was the next planned attack on a Member of Parliament (MP). This precipitated the arrest and prevention of the planned attack on Rosie Cooper MP.

After leaving the police, I set up an advisory service called Defuse Global, and now provide the same expertise to public figures, private clients and organizations worldwide, demystifying the world of security and protective intelligence, and helping them to feel safer.

Throughout my early life and then my career, I was drawn to helping people who felt vulnerable, often from bullies causing physical, reputational or psychological harm. These vulnerable people were anxious, often anticipating an attack of some sort. The common denominator has been that physical security measures have often failed to make them feel safer.

To help people feel safer, I had to learn how to solve the problem that was causing them to feel unsafe rather than apply a sticking plaster to provide a short-term solution.

I have worked with many public figures, some household names, others global business leaders, including Middle Eastern royalty. They tell me that they often feel increasingly anxious, unable to know who to trust and, when threatened online and offline, this can make them feel more paranoid and fearful. This can be exacerbated when their security increases due to the understandable assumption that they are in increased danger from the threats made. It is a common misconception by many who assume that directly communicated threats illustrate an increased danger.

Introduction

Rarely a day goes by when the media fail to report a story of a death threat being directed at a public or prominent figure.

The challenge is identifying which threats are real and which are designed to create fear, be abusive and intimidate.

There is a difference between those who abuse, threaten and intimate, and those who pose a real threat. The vast majority will be what we call 'Howlers'. They are the trolls who abuse people and often will occupy much of the client's time and energy. But the truth is they rarely pose a real threat.

This book seeks to demystify the subject, clarify some terminology, and explain how and why someone might pose a threat. I want you to be better informed to make better decisions about your own and your client's safety.

This book is intended as a practitioner's guide. While it isn't an academic book, I have referenced several academic studies should you wish to delve deeper and read the research material.

Part 1 explains some terms we, as security practitioners, use, such as *threat*, *risk* and *vulnerability*. You may have heard them, but do you really understand them? This is critical for two reasons: first, so you understand what I mean as I use these terms throughout the book; and second, because only when you understand the terms can you mitigate the issues.

Part 2 of the book is about managing the threats you have probably been tasked with dealing with. It explains the different types of threats, which ones are more serious, and why. The final piece of the puzzle is about how to be safer: I want you to know what I know.

Throughout the book, I will use case studies, all of which are based on real stories. However, to protect the privacy of my clients, names, identifying facts and details have been altered so that none of these examples depicts any real person, dead or alive. Some famous cases have been publicly reported and are used to emphasize lessons to be learned.

In 2021, I began my podcast called The Defuse Podcast (formerly called The Online Bodyguard®, a name the UK media gave me despite never having been a bodyguard).[2] Through this podcast, I have had the opportunity to dive deeper with global experts, many of whom have published the research this book will cover. They have discussed cases they have worked on, sharing their expertise and the nuggets of wisdom that can only be learned through years of practical experience.

This book passes on that wisdom, introducing it to you, tasked with protecting some of the most well-known, important and wealthy people on the planet.

By the end of this book, you will understand that there are different types of stalkers, each motivated to pose a different threat. You will know how to triage a communicated threat and when to call in a specialist. You will better understand how those who target your clients operate and how to mitigate the threats they pose. You will better understand how vulnerable you and your clients are, and what steps to take to reduce that.

Most of all, my aim is that you find this book useful, keep referring to it as a guide, and use it to help your clients feel safer.

PART 1

Understanding the threats

Part 1 covers the causes and theories with regards to the threats that you and your clients may be faced with.

We start the book with defining some of the terms that are used in the book. You may already have some knowledge of these terms and know the basis of the subjects covered. For you to get the most out of the book, understanding these terms is critical and while you may use different definitions, please accept mine while reading this book.

There are difficult types of threats; each chapter goes into greater detail and uses case studies to provide clarity to explain the foundations, the research behind the understanding, and the level of threat and risk posed.

What is critical to understand with this book is that the harm that is posed can be multi-dimensional. It is often the case that harm focuses on the physical or violent harm. However, in many cases the harm may be psychological, financial or reputational, and no physical harm may be threatened or caused. In my experience this is one of the issues that causes difficulties for law enforcement when they are asked to investigate, as the non-physical threatened are often hard to define and are not always tangible. The important of these different types of harm and the impact they have can still be life changing.

I believe that to counter a threat, it is helpful to understand what that is, how it manifests, and in some cases the psychology behind those who are involved. This essence is the diagnosis phase of the book, and in a similar vain to a medical doctor, without this understanding I don't believe you can be truly effective in developing the tactics required to help clients feel safer.

Part 1 of this book is designed to provide you with a good foundation before you move on the Part 2: solving the problem.

Chapter 1

Security vs safety

Introduction

*S*ecurity is a term we are all familiar with. It is used in various contexts, from state security to food security, and has been the subject of detailed research by a growing cadre of academics.

Security forms part of our everyday language. Most of us are now familiar with our smartphone's security settings and the concept of cyber security. Increasingly, wherever we go, we encounter some form of physical security. A simplified explanation is that security is there to prevent bad things from happening to us. This book is specifically about personal safety and protective security.

The difference between security and safety

Safety and *security* are often used together or confused as the same thing. In this section, I'll discuss what these terms mean, how they interact, and how they can be improved.

According to the Cambridge Dictionary, security is the 'protection of a person, building, organization, or country against threats such as crime or attacks by foreign countries', while safety is defined as' a state of being protected from danger or harm'.[3]

In simple terms, we might argue that safety is a feeling, while security is a physical action.

Safety as a feeling is key because without it, performance drops.

You can ensure your home is 100% secure by installing the right windows and doors, properly functioning locks, alarm systems and all the other elements of home security. Despite that, you may still feel unsafe. You may find yourself as part of a full close protection team, but your clients may still feel unsafe and, in many cases, the more security they have, the less safe they feel. They might assume that because they are provided with so much security, they must be in significant danger and feel unsafe.

Safety and security are not always aligned. When staying in a hotel, your clients may have been advised to use a doorstop to prevent anyone from forcing their door open. However, that advice may contravene health and safety and delay the fire service entering your room if there is a fire, causing them to be less safe.

A business may open the fire doors in the event of an alarm to ensure a speedy evacuation, allowing an intruder unfettered access to the building to commit a crime.

One of the by-products of being in the public eye is the constant attention it attracts. When someone is thrust into the spotlight, they may attract 'unwanted' attention. That unwanted attention can develop into overly intrusive and even stalking behaviour, which I will expand on and define in Chapter 2. You may have already experienced this, and with that comes the feelings of paranoia and hypervigilance. These emotions may cause them to feel constantly unsafe, repeatedly scanning for threats even when none exist. This constant feeling of being unsafe is draining and will cause them to lose sleep, change their decision-making and act differently. It might be argued that safety is a perception rather than a reality; it's an internal experience.

This was apparent when I looked after MPs in the UK Parliament during the Brexit debates as the UK planned to leave the European

Union. Despite working in a secure site with armed police officers and a dedicated policing team, some MPs felt unsafe due to the volume and toxicity of abuse they were receiving. This then caused some to question how they were going to vote on a Brexit debate, as they felt that by voting with their conscience, they'd attract further abuse and threats. I tackled this by explaining some of what this book will contain and how those who make direct threats rarely pose a real threat. These threats are often just noise rather than signs of an impending incident. I encouraged them to listen to my expertise rather than well-meaning friends and colleagues.

These feelings of being unsafe were understandably increased following the murder of Jo Cox MP, despite the level of security having increased significantly. Jo Cox was a Labour MP representing the constituency of Batley and Spen in Yorkshire. She was pro-European Union and pro-immigration. She was a moderated MP who passionately believed in inclusivity. She was not high profile, nor did she express or hold any controversial views that would increase the risks to her. On 16 June 2016, during the early debates concerning Brexit, she was killed after being attacked on the street outside a meeting she was due to attend. She was shot and stabbed multiple times by Thomas Mair.

Thomas Mair is a white supremacist obsessed with the belief that white people were facing an existential threat from immigrants. His home was reportedly full of Nazi and racist memorabilia. He was known to have subscribed to several publications supporting the South African apartheid regime, among others. However, he had a special hatred of white people who supported campaigns against the very things he believed in. He considered them to be 'the collaborators'. As part of the Brexit campaign, extreme right-wing movements made claims that Brexit would result in mass immigration and a further threat to 'white people'.[4] It was Mair's pathological fixation on anti-immigration and white supremacy that caused him to see Jo Cox MP as a threat, a threat he eliminated.

I remember being first posted to Northern Ireland as a young soldier fresh out of The Guard's Depot. I arrived at Belfast International Airport and was driven from there to where I would be based. The general feeling among our group was one of apprehension and expectancy of seeing bomb craters and soldiers everywhere. We were being deployed as 'security forces'; my perceptions were quite different from reality. Initially, I felt scared, as if armed gunmen would immediately confront me. I felt safer and less scared as I became more experienced. Nothing had changed except my perceptions, feelings and skills. The levels of security hadn't changed. I had.

The murder of Sarah Everard (kidnapped and murdered by a policeman) has had a significant impact on how safe some women feel in the UK. In that specific case, the very people they should be able to trust, the police, had, betrayed that trust and became the monster they feared. That incident was followed by several others which further damaged the trust the police previously enjoyed, causing some women to publicly state they would not approach or trust a male police officer in the event of an emergency. When trust in the police breaks down, it becomes a significant security issue.

The key to safety and security is to find a balance where they act in harmony, supporting each other.

In this book, I will discuss some of the threats you may have already experienced and had to manage. By explaining them and separating the myths from the facts, I hope to change your perspectives. With some advice on how to reduce vulnerabilities, you will experience a change in tackling these issues.

Threat, vulnerability and *risk*: what do they mean?

In this section, I want to ensure you understand some of the common terms you may be aware of or hear about but may not fully understand.

These terms are important because only by understanding them can you use them effectively. The key terms I will explain are *threat*, *vulnerability* and *risk*.

Most people use the term *risk*, often in different contexts. What is a risk?

Risk is the possible harm that may occur if we do nothing to counter it. We measure risks by comparing how likely something is to happen and then assessing the impact or harm if it were to occur.

As an example, let me take you back to the COVID-19 pandemic[5] in the UK. When travelling on the train or other public transport, despite being mandated, I would see some people wearing face masks and others choosing not to do so.

Without consciously realizing it, they had all conducted a risk assessment. They had assessed the likelihood (*vulnerability*) of catching COVID-19 (*threat*) if they chose not to wear a face mask and the impact on their health should they catch it.

Those who decided they were likely to catch COVID-19, and that the impact would be high, were more likely to wear a face mask.

Conversely, those who had chosen not to wear a mask had assessed that the likelihood of catching it was low (or non-existent in those who considered the pandemic a conspiracy theory) and/or that the impact would be low or non-existent. Therefore, they assessed the risk by using the combination of likelihood and impact.

We can see this being conducted in everyday experiences, from simple examples such as whether to cross the road to the more complex question of whether it is safe to go outdoors. Almost every decision that is made involves a risk assessment.

If I choose to take that job, what is the likelihood of my success/failure, and what will the financial/success/reputational impact be?

The interesting thing about risk is that our assessment can change with experience and exposure. I have spent most of my life working in risky environments, such as the army and the police. I consider that I have a high 'risk tolerance'. That means I am happy to accept a higher level of risk than those with a lower tolerance. My tolerance is based on my experiences and my knowledge. I have spent over 30 years dealing with crime, including terrorism, murders, child abuse, domestic violence and acquisitive crime. If my tolerance was much lower, then I may be unable to operate in a high risk environment, as I'd assess that it is too dangerous to leave the building.

The problem with that is that because of my level of tolerance, I may miscalculate and accept a risk that I shouldn't. That is a risk I take when making decisions, but because of my experience I assess that the likelihood of me getting it wrong is low and the impact will be negligent. That is because when making decisions, I think consciously about them and have lots of reference points to assess my decisions against.

Likelihood + Impact (harm) = Risk

The term *threat* involves an external issue that has the potential to cause harm.

Threats are a combination of intent and capability. For a threat to be genuine, someone must have both the intent and capability to cause harm.

If someone in Australia posts a threat on social media to someone in England, they may have the intent but because of the distance they don't have the immediate capability, so any threat can be dismissed. Equally, should the sender's intent be to scare or intimidate, then whatever their capability, there is no threat of violence, just intimidation.

The same assessment is made when a national threat level is published. As I write this, the published threat to the UK (England, Wales, Scotland and Northern Ireland) from terrorism is SUBSTANTIAL.

This means that all the available intelligence has been assessed, and the intent of those seeking to harm the UK, together with their capability of successfully conducting an attack, is considered substantial. The threat level is set as substantial, which means that an attack is likely.

To qualify this, I will compare the two following threat assessments.

1. Does the USA have the capability to successfully attack the UK? Answer: Yes. But does it have the necessary intent? Answer: (hopefully) No! Therefore, the threat from the USA is Low (which means an attack is highly unlikely).
2. Does one of our major enemies have the capacity to attack the UK? Answer: Yes. Do they have the necessary intent? Answer: Yes! Therefore, the threat from our enemy is higher. The level of the threat will then depend on an assessment of their capability and intent.

In his excellent book *The Rules of Security*, Paul Martin provides a more precise definition, stating that 'a threat is a probability that threat actors will make a credible attempt to attack', suggesting that the attempt reflects the intention and the attack the capability.[6]

$$\text{Intent} + \text{Capability} = \text{Threat}$$

The term *vulnerability* involves the gaps and weaknesses that exist when confronted by a threat. The level of vulnerability is constantly changing and can depend on various factors, often context driven.

For example, when you are tired and on your way home from work, you may be less focused and more vulnerable to being a victim of a crime.

Equally, if, as part of a Public Relations (PR) campaign, you decide to invite a magazine into your home to film and photograph where you live and highlight some of your most valuable possessions, you are making yourself more vulnerable to being a victim of a burglary.

Adversaries, be they someone you're in a dispute with, criminals or terrorists, are constantly looking for vulnerabilities to exploit.

When conducting any assessment, I am looking to assess the current level and then reduce it.

Managing threat and risk

By now, you will better understand the key terms used in security and safety. We now know that *risk = threat + vulnerability*. This next section will progress us along the journey and share how to manage the threats and risks identified.

Security risk management is the ongoing process of identifying security risks and implementing plans to address them. Threat assessment and management are the processes of identifying, assessing and managing threats. Therefore, it is key to understand the threat to manage any personal risks.

I can have lots of intent, but without the required capability, it means nothing. If I recognize that someone has the necessary intent, perhaps caused by a grievance, I can focus on trying to resolve that to make the threat go away.

If I am unable to do that, I must then focus on tackling their capabilities. This may cause them to be arrested so they cannot carry out their threat, ensure they can't get close to me, or make sure that I focus on closing what gaps I may have in my security. We do this via a vulnerability assessment.

If I can either resolve their intent or reduce their capability to attack, I can then reduce or remove the threat.

To manage risk, we first must identify the threats and vulnerabilities that create the risk we want to mitigate.

Within the subject of risk management, there are numerous different models, often specific to the industry involved.

Most models accept that not every risk can be reduced or removed and that some level of risk may have to be accepted. If we fail to accept risk, we might never go out, as everyday life will always involve some risk. This is a called residual risk.

For some, the risk they experience is a perception rather than a reality. However, that is irrelevant to them, as to them it is real. This can be seen in those who develop a level of paranoia when they feel targeted.

To complete a proper risk management plan, you must identify all the possible risks and develop a strategy for dealing with each one. The risks must then be recorded either manually or on a risk management platform, of which there are many.

If you haven't prepared a risk management plan, it may be well worth asking to see one. If someone else's plan hasn't considered all the potential risks of any situation, that is a problem. One of the first things the Health and Safety Executive will do in the event of any accident is to request to see the recorded strategy.

Another useful method is to create a risk matrix or register. A risk register is a live risk management tool used to collect potential risk events, organize them by risk categories, and assign responsibility to who will own them. It also serves as a place to include additional information about each risk, like the nature of the risk and how it will be handled. This is hugely useful when you have identified a risk that you cannot avoid and yet are not given or do not have the resources to manage it. By registering the risk, it becomes an accepted residual risk that still requires attention.

The RARA Risk Assessment Model

RARA is a simple model of personal safety that I use. It was introduced some years ago and is primarily used regarding domestic violence.

The RARA Model =

>   **R**educe

>   **A**ccept

>   **R**emove

>   **A**void

When I was responsible for protecting the safety of Members of Parliament (MPs) from threats, I would use this model. Using RARA would look something like this:

How can I **reduce** the likelihood of an MP being targeted and physically attacked?

I could conduct a vulnerability assessment on their home and their offices. This helps to understand any gaps in the security, and then I can advise them what protective security measures they require to reduce the likelihood that an adversary can gain access.

What level of risk is **acceptable**?

Politicians must operate in public. Advising that they never attend a meeting where they might be challenged would not be plausible, as that would infringe on democracy. Therefore, I can accept that they will be challenged and possibly shouted at, as I am aware that the likelihood of that turning violent is low.

How can I **remove** the risk they are exposed to?

By removing certain private information from public databases, I can remove the risk of their home addresses being identified.

How can I help politicians **avoid** certain risk?

By providing them with specific advice and guidance on how to run their constituency surgeries, I can help them avoid the risk of being attacked.

Let's change tack and be relatable to you. Imagine you are travelling home from a night out. Your goal is to arrive home safely. You have waved goodbye to your friends and left the city centre bar you've been in. The train station is a 5-minute walk away.

To **reduce** any real or perceived risks, you might get a pre-booked taxi to the station or ask a friend to escort you there.

Because of the time of night, there are some people out and about who are drunk. There is a level of risk you **accept** at the time of night in any city centre, but you can choose a route to **avoid** groups of drunk people and empty streets.

To **remove** the risks altogether, you could ask a friend to pick you up from the venue and drive you all the way home.

The same exercise can be used in various circumstances, including those outside of personal safety.

The key to any risk management process is that information is constantly changing and, therefore, so are the risks, which require constant review.

In the example you have just read, let's suppose that as you begin to walk towards the train station, you bump into a friend who lives near you and suggests that you travel home together or perhaps share a taxi home, the whole risk assessment then changes.

The National Decision-Making Model

In UK policing, a National Decision-Making Model (NDM) is used. Officers are encouraged to use the NDM to structure a rationale of what they did during an incident and why. This model is a continuous process in which officers constantly review the information they know, and the risks involved.

A perfectly good decision about a risky situation can be made, and within 5 minutes, because of new information, that decision would no longer be the correct choice, so I would then change my decision.

Every risk management process must be constant, and any decision you make must only be correct with the information you have. Never be scared to change your mind when the information changes.

Figure 1.1: The National Decision-Making Model

I might walk into a quiet street and feel quite safe. Within minutes, a group of people enters the street from the other end. I must then review my risk assessment with this new information. My initial decision may be correct and, equally, it may need refreshing. Flexibility is the key.

As a final thought, there is a theory among practitioners that there is no such thing as 'low risk'. The argument is that if you are unaware of anything that may escalate or mitigate the risks, you are left with an 'unknown risk'.

Targeted or intended attacks

Targeted or intended attacks are determined, purposeful and often emotionless. In this section, I'll explain what a targeted or intended attack is and how it differs from the other types of attacks. This is relevant to you because public and high profile figures are subjected to such attacks, and they are conducted in quite specific ways, often leaving clues.

The term *attack*, while recognized as an aggressive or violent act against a person or place, can also refer to any targeted act, such as one designed to destroy a person's reputation, cause them to fear or intimidate them.

Regarding the subject of physical violence, there are two types. There is affective or impulsive violence, and predatory or targeted violence.

Affective or impulsive violence is, as the name suggests, impulsive. This type of violence is driven by emotions and will include domestic violence, as well as alcohol- or drug-fuelled violence such as a pub fight, road rage or an incident at work following an argument. This is where someone snaps or reacts to a situation. Research has identified that this type of violence is preceded by *autonomic arousal* and is triggered by some perceived external threat together with a sense of anger or fear. The picture of a cat backed into a corner, teeth bared, snarling back on its haunches, ready to attack, is synonymous with affective violence.

Targeted or intended violence is quite different. While there may be emotions at the root of the issue, such as from a grievance, the actual act of violence is not emotional. It might be considered cold and calculated. There is evidence that some of the attackers take anti-anxiety drugs to ensure they remain calm during the attack. Targeted or intended violence is driven by thoughts or fantasies, such as revenge.

Targeted or intended violence is also referred to as predatory or goal-driven violence because there is little or no autonomic arousal or emotion in the person responsible. The person doesn't feel subject to any immediate threat; they are not reacting to some external issue. This type of violence is predatory and, therefore, takes time to plan. They don't just snap; they plan, prepare, identify the vulnerability as their target and attack when ready. It is because of this strategy that they often leave clues. Some will get huge satisfaction from the 'hunting' phase of the planned attack.

Targeted or intended violence is directed at specific individuals, groups or locations. Targeted or intended violence may include terrorist attacks and the targeting of public figures. According to the University of Nebraska's Targeted Violence research team, these types of violence include sexual assault, stalking, threatening behaviours and extremist activity.[7]

Targeted or intended violence and attacks are especially concerning to a public figure or someone with a public profile. History is littered with successful attacks on prominent figures (such as the murder of Jo Cox MP, referred to earlier in this book) and have been the subject of significant research. They also take different forms. While much of the research and this book refer to physical attacks, psychological and

reputational attacks are increasingly prevalent.

The person responsible plans their attack. They will spend days, weeks, months and, in extreme cases, years researching the subject of their intended attack. They look for patterns of behaviour and vulnerabilities they can exploit. They act as predators. In contrast to the cornered cat, this is more like a large cat hunting down its prey.

Because such attacks are predatory, a target's predicable behaviour is most vulnerable. This is especially relevant to those in public life.

Targeted or intended violence is not purely focused on physical violence. It can also be focused on general crime. There are numerous examples of prominent figures who have been targeted for acquisitive crime. You are probably familiar with the accounts of celebrity Kim Kardashian's robbery in Paris,[8] footballer John Terry's burglary at his home while he was away on holiday[9] or the boxer Amir Khan's gunpoint robbery of his £70,000 watch.[10]

None of these crimes were random; each was very targeted. For these prominent people to be targeted, their location and their high value assets must be known. Many of the criminals who target prominent people research them on the internet, where some public figures show off their possessions for all to see.

In addition to targeting people, specific venues can also be targeted. Some of these venues are high-net-worth venues such as luxury restaurants, bars and clubs. These are targeted because the assumption is that the clientele will have an ultra-high net worth. Other venues may be targeted because of bias that exists among the person targeting them. These venues may be chosen based on the race, religion or sexual preferences of those who attend them. Two examples of this include the attack on the Finsbury Park Mosque in London by Darren Osborne,[11] in which the extreme right-wing terrorist drove a vehicle at a crowd of worshipers, killing one and injuring several others. In 1999, the Admiral Duncan bar in Soho, London, was one of a series of attacks by David Copeland, as it was frequented by the LGBTQ+ community.[12]

Over the past few years, we have seen similar targeted attacks on schools, workplaces and public spaces like shopping centres. Some of these attacks were committed by marginalized groups such as incels,[13] while others were extremist-driven terrorist attacks.

Summary

This first chapter has introduced you to some of the key terms relating to personal security and safety. You will have learned that *security* is the 'protection of a person, building, organization, or country against threats such as crime or attacks by foreign countries', while *safety* is defined as 'a state of being protected from danger or harm'. That leads us to the meanings of *risk*, *threat* and *vulnerability*, and how they are connected. This is important because unless you understand what the terms mean and the component parts, it is very difficult to know how to mitigate them. Once you understand the meaning, you can manage them better. Risk and threat management are as relevant to you as they are to governments who conduct the same assessments. I then introduced the concept of being *targeted*. People may be targeted because of who they are, the people they spend time with or the places they go. The key to mitigating such threats is to manage the information that is shared and made publicly available.

Chapter 2

Fixated threats

Introduction

This chapter will discuss the threats posed by people who become fixated. People vary in their fixation, from obsessing about specific people, often referred to as 'superfans', to those who obsess about an ideology or cause.

History is littered with cases in which a fixated person has targeted someone – resulting, in some instances, in a physical, sometimes fatal attack. Recently, it has become fashionable to attack others to destroy their reputations.

In this chapter, I will explain the motivation of fixated people, how they pose a threat, and their different methodologies. I will illustrate their behaviour and the risks they pose using both recent and historical examples.

Fixated people

Fixated people is a broad term for those individuals who become pathologically fixated on another, a cause or those who represent a cause.

Fixated people very often leak their obsession through their behaviour. This section will explain who they are, the differences between the typologies, and the threats they pose.

The first thing to explain is what it means when someone is fixated. Many people experience some form of fixation during their lives. You may encounter this when you meet a new intimate partner, take up a new activity, or follow a sports team, musician or band. In most cases, that 'fixation' is temporary and manageable. By that, it means it doesn't take over your life. You can still function, work and enjoy a normal life.

In this chapter, the people referred to as fixated are considered pathologically fixated. *Pathological* means they behave in an extreme and unacceptable way and have very powerful feelings that they cannot control.

Fixated persons are those who hold pathologically intense fixations on individuals or causes, and these are often pursued to an abnormally intense degree.[14]

Pathologically fixated people can spend every waking moment of their day obsessing about their fixation. That fixation completely takes over their lives.

It is because of this preoccupation that they can become so dangerous. The role of mental illness in the activities of fixated persons is well known. Meloy and Amman's (2016) study showed that 44.8% of offenders were known to have a mental health problem (36% unknown).[15] A majority (86%) of those assessed by London's Fixated Threat Assessment Centre, a joint Police and medical professional team set up to manage those individuals who became fixated on the UK Royal Family, were diagnosed with a psychotic disorder.[16] Indeed, mental illness has been identified among those who inappropriately target different types of public figures and those associated with them. However, it is critical to recognize that not all people with a fixation are mentally ill, and not all mentally ill people become fixated.

Fixated people can present a significant security issue. Due to the nature of their fixation, they can spend all day and night researching the subject of their obsession. If they become fixated on someone you are protecting, they likely know more about them, their routine, likes and dislikes, and the security protocols in place than anyone. They are often very adept at investigating the internet, becoming open-source experts, and identifying vulnerabilities in any security plan.

One element of fixated people that can cause issues is their desire for proximity. They want and need to get close. When this desire for proximity is thwarted, either by security or by the limitations in their own capabilities (such as lacking the funds to travel), it can create a deep feeling of anger and has been known to hijack their lives emotionally. This can be the trigger for them to act on their anger.

As mentioned, there are two main areas of fixation. The first is those who become fixated on a person.

There is no singular reason for a fixation. Some people become fixated on a celebrity or on the character that a celebrity plays. Others may become fixated on a business leader or person with whom they desire an intimate relationship. An extreme example of this was John Hinkley Jr.

Many people will know John Hinkley Jr as the man who attacked US President Ronald Reagan in March 1981 as he left a hotel in Washington DC. Hinkley Jr fired six shots at President Reagan. One round ricocheted off the side of the President's vehicle, while three other rounds hit individuals working with him, including a police officer, a US Secret Service Agent and a press secretary. The press secretary, James Brady, was critically injured and later died from his injuries.

What many would not be so familiar with was the motivation behind the attack on Reagan. It had very little to do with Reagan or politics. Hinckley shot Reagan because he had been fixated on the actress Jodie Foster since 1976. Before leaving his hotel to attack Reagan, Hinckley wrote a letter to Foster in which he said:

Over the past seven months, I've left you dozens of poems, letters and love messages in the faint hope that you could develop an interest in me. Although we talked on the phone a couple of times, I never had the nerve to simply approach you and introduce myself... The reason I'm going ahead with this attempt now is that I cannot wait any longer to impress you.... By sacrificing my freedom and possibly my life, I hope to change your mind about me. This letter is being written an hour before I leave for the Hilton Hotel. Jodie, I'm asking you to please look into your heart and at least give me the chance with this historical deed to gain your respect and love. I love you forever. [signed] John Hinckley.[17]

It is important to recognize that the violence was not targeted at the focus of his fixation. It was his delusions that caused him to believe his actions would impress Jodie Foster.

Another reason people fixate is their obsession with an ideology or cause. Often, a person is targeted as a by-product or representation of the ideology, such as a politician or a celebrity who may be involved in a campaign that counters that cause. Increasingly, this typology can be witnessed in the attacks by what have been termed *lone actors* involved in terrorist attacks.

These causes or ideologies can range from extreme right-wing white supremacist groups and extreme Islamist fundamentalists, such as ISIS[18] and Al-Qaeda[19] to single-issue groups such as anti-abortionist, environmental and animal rights groups. Not everyone involved in these groups will necessarily be described as 'fixated', albeit it can be suggested that their very association involves some form of obsessional behaviour. However, at the extremes of any of these groups, you can expect to find pathologically fixated ones.

As we learned earlier in this book, Jo Cox MP was not high profile, nor did she express or hold any controversial views that would increase the risks to her. Yet 16 June 2016, during the early debates concerning Brexit,[20] she was shot and stabbed multiple times by Thomas Mair.[21]

To reiterate, Mair was a white supremacist whose home was reportedly full of Nazi and racist memorabilia. He was known to have subscribed to several publications supporting the South African apartheid regime, among others. However, he had a special hatred of white people who supported campaigns against the very things he believed in. He considered them to be 'the collaborators'. As part of the Brexit campaign, extreme right-wing movements made claims that Brexit would result in mass immigration and a further threat to 'white people'. It was Mair's pathological fixation on anti-immigration and white supremacy that caused him to see Jo Cox MP as a threat, a threat he eliminated.

In both extreme examples, we have a person who acted on an obsessional and irrational pathological fixation, which enabled them to think the killing was going to advance their belief.

Fixated people are pathological, consumed by their own obsessional thinking, and some are driven to act on these beliefs.

Grievances

This section is about *grievances*. We have all heard of them; most companies have a grievance policy. Grievances are the basis of most disputes and targeted attacks. This section will delve deeper into this topic, explaining how they motivate these attacks, the causes behind the grievances and how you might deal with them.

Significant research exists on grievance-fuelled violence. As a manager, I have always been aware of the term and have been involved in grievance procedures. However, I didn't realize that grievances are the root cause of most disputes and can be broadly grouped into one of four categories.

You may have seen or heard of 'manifestos' of terrorists on the news. I can recall watching the videos of the 7/7 London bombers on the news (2005) with the black Islamist flag as a backdrop. In those videos, they laid out their grievances as a justification for their murderous campaign. The ringleader of the attack, Mohammed Siddique Khan, stated:

> Your democratically elected governments continuously perpetuate atrocities against my people, and your support of them makes you directly responsible, just as I am directly responsible for protecting and avenging my Muslim brothers and sisters.

> Until we feel security, you will be our target. Until you stop the bombing, gassing, imprisonment and torture of my people, we will not stop this fight.

From this brief section of his video, his grievance was blame and anger. He blamed the British Government for the atrocities and anger at the way he perceived 'his' people were treated.

In their article titled 'Rethinking the Path to Intended Violence', Calhoun and Weston state 'fear and hatred of the "other", individuals or groups, different from those feeling the fear and hatred, spawns violence.[22]

In his interview on my podcast,[23] Dr Reid Meloy suggested that personal grievances have four elements to them:

- blame
- loss
- anger, and
- humiliation.

The common denominator is that the person of concern feels that they are the victim of an injustice. Let me give you four quick examples:

Blame: If the mortgage company repossesses your home because you couldn't afford to pay it after losing your job, you might blame your former boss for sacking you and form a grievance against them.

Loss: If a drunk driver kills a family member and doesn't receive long enough in custody, you might form a grievance against the judge for failing to recognize your loss.

Anger: If your partner ends your relationship and demands 50% of your assets in the separation, your anger might become a grievance.

Humiliation: You feel humiliated when your boss sacked you and made you leave the office carrying a cardboard box full of your possessions in front of your colleagues. Your grievance may be against the boss or the company.

If you eliminate any of these four elements, you may mitigate a personal grievance.

The grievance may make no rational sense to anyone other than the person involved, but to them it is very real. It may be that nothing you do will resolve that, however unreasonable that is to you. The key to this is that the subject's opinion counts.

A grievance that forms a violent ideation is caused by their inability to resolve that grievance. The attacker believes that they have run out of ideas and, therefore, their only remedy to resolve the issue is through violence.

A further motivation to target public and famous figures has been the attacker's desire for notoriety. They may feel angry at their perceived irrelevance and see others getting all the attention and praise with rewards they believe they deserve. Their attack satisfies that anger and will forever be associated with the person they attacked, increasing their relevance. If you search online for John Lennon, his killer, Mark Chapman, is associated with any searches you conduct. This desire for notoriety can also be seen in attacks on venues and places of note.

When dealing with someone who has a grievance, the challenge is to differentiate angry people from dangerous ones. You will undoubtedly encounter friends, colleagues or adversaries who have grievances; we all have them; we just don't all act on them.

Grievances can be deep-rooted or recently embedded. Unresolved, they can be the driving force behind a devastating targeted attack. This can be problematic when trying to distinguish who to focus on. Some of us may form a grievance that is quickly resolved or forgotten while others last a lifetime.

This is where the subject of behavioural threat analysis[24] comes in. While a grievance is mentally constructed, it is only through observing behaviours that we identify those who appear to be escalating and seeking revenge.

Case study

A corporate client (an employer) was being subjected to threats from a person of concern who had a grievance against them. Their family member took their own life some time after leaving the employer. The inquest found no connection between the act and the employer. However, the person of concern blamed the company and made several unfounded accusations and unreasonable demands. Their behaviour identified that they were escalating as they began to make threats to key members of the Board. They did this by repeated phone calls, emails and other forms of correspondence. The reporting of their behaviour to the police only triggered a further escalation. Their behaviour caused fear and anxiety in those they targeted. They began a stalking campaign, referencing where individuals lived, having conducted online research. Ultimately, they were arrested and dealt with by the police. However, their grievances remain unresolved.

The amount of time and energy this person of concern had invested in their grievance suggests that they won't just 'go away'; they rarely do.

Grievances such as this have increasingly been seen in a new typology labelled *lone actors*. Lone actors have been described as isolated individuals with intense social grievances and vendettas triggered by some form of injustice. The behaviours seen in these lone actors mirror those witnessed in other groups involved in fixated and targeted groups, such that in many cases, they can be treated as one group.

Summary

The threat from individuals with a fixation can be a complex subject. In simple terms we are dealing with people who have an obsession that has taken over their lives. The nature of that obsession can be a person and their relationship with them – be that an intimate relationship, a professional relationship or a delusional one – or it can be associated with a cause or ideology such as the environment, a religion or a race. Their fixation can be caused by a real or perceived grievance in which they feel they are the subject of an injustice. While it is a deeply emotional attachment, they rarely just snap. They crave proximity so will often approach the person, a venue or a representative of the cause they have issue with, and this is often where they become a security issue.

Chapter 3

Unwanted attention

Introduction

The terms *stalking* and *harassment* are widely used but rarely properly understood. In the UK, this is partly due to poorly written legislation and a lack of agreed definitions. Both stalking and harassment are invasive crimes that can cause a deep sense of fear, harm and paranoia. Both crimes have escalated rapidly with the growing exposure to the internet and social media. This section explains what both offences will look like to you, how to protect your clients from them and what to do when they are targeted.

The first thing to recognize is that both harassment and stalking require a 'course of conduct'. That means there must be at least two incidents of unwanted communication or attention. The more it happens, the more serious it may be considered. Evidentially, the closer together the incidents are, the stronger the evidence, but a gap between them doesn't always negate there being a case that can be prosecuted.

Harassment

Harassment includes repeated attempts to impose 'unwanted communications and contact' which are likely to cause distress or fear. It must be targeted at a person (or a group) and the person harassing is likely to know that they are harassing the person they are targeting. Naturally, they are likely to deny they knew that what they were doing was harassment, so this excuse is removed by the addition of the term *ought to know*. Good evidence of this is that you can prove you have asked that the unwanted communication stops but they continue to communicate. This can be evidenced by a message back to them asking them to stop, by a 'cease and desist' letter or when that request is communicated verbally, have someone witnessing that communication is beneficial.

In real terms, this may be unwanted emails, text messages, phone calls, letters or gifts sent that cause distress. A person can harass you even if they don't know who the recipient is, or by them communicating to a third party referencing the recipient. One of the challenges is that the UK legislation was passed before the emergence of social media and, as such, the legislation fails to mention or tackle the use of social media to cause harassment. There is an excuse or defence for harassment, when the contact is for a lawful purpose, such as collecting a debt or enforcing a law.

Stalking

The Suzy Lamplugh Trust,[26] a leading stalking authority, was set up following the disappearance and believed murder of estate agent Suzy Lamplugh in 1986. The Trust has defined stalking as 'a pattern of fixated and obsessive behaviour which is repeated, persistent, intrusive and causes fear of violence or engenders alarm and distress in the victim'.

The Crown Prosecution Service, the prosecuting agency in the UK, has suggested that stalking includes the following behaviours:

- following a person
- contacting, or attempting to contact, a person by any means
- publishing any statement or other material relating or purporting to relate to a person, or purporting to originate from a person

- monitoring the use by a person of the internet, email or any other form of electronic communication
- loitering in any place (whether public or private)
- interfering with any property in the possession of a person
- watching or spying on a person.[27]

In simple terms, stalking is when one person follows another, watching or spying on them, or forcing contact with them through any means, including social media. The effect of this behaviour is to cause someone to change their behaviour because they feel they are being watched and because that feeling of being watched causes that person to be fearful. Think of how you'd understand an animal stalking its prey, which goes some way to understanding stalking.

One critical difference between *stalking* and *harassment* is that stalkers are significantly more dangerous, stalking behaviour has been identified in a number of murder investigations.[28]

A common acronym used to define stalking is FOUR:

Fixated
Obsessive
Unwanted
Repeated

In general terms, roughly 80% of victims of stalking are female. This doesn't mean that men don't get stalked; they do. In terms of those who stalk, 86% are men, but it is important to recognize that all sexes can be both victims and perpetrators.

Types of this behaviour may include:

1. unwanted or malicious communication
2. assaults
3. unwanted attention from somebody seeking a romantic relationship

4. violent predatory behaviour
5. sending unwanted gifts
6. persistently following someone
7. repeatedly going uninvited to their home
8. monitoring someone's use of the internet, email or other form of electronic communication
9. loitering somewhere frequented by the person
10. interfering with or damaging their property
11. watching or spying on someone, and/or
12. identity theft.

Much is made of cyber stalking, which in my view is misleading as almost all harassment and stalking now involves use of the internet. However, there are some specific ways in which they may target a person online, including:

- identity theft
- posting false profiles online
- publishing material relating to you online
- direct threats through digital means, e.g. texts, messages, phone calls, faxes, social media, and/or
- using technology to track someone.

Stalking can occur over short periods or over years and even decades, so any investigation must be seen as a possible long-term investment and the 'stalker' might be considered to have stopped when in fact they have just paused. Stalkers rarely just stop! It is for this reason that any risk assessment must be subject to a regular and an ongoing review. It is critical that any investigation is properly managed and in some cases is subject to a peer review to ensure that nothing is missed.

Another challenge with stalkers is that they often move their focus from their initial target to others, such as the investigator, lawyer or friend who is seen to intervene.

Types of stalkers

One of the challenges with stalking investigations is that stalkers are often seen as a homogonous group of individuals. This is a dangerous approach to take as they and their motives can be quite different and the risks they pose can differ too.

In 1999, a key piece of research titled 'Study of Stalkers' was conducted.[29]

Five types of stalkers were identified, each driven by a different motivation.

1. The **Rejected Stalker** commences stalking after the breakdown of an important relationship that was usually, but not always, sexually intimate in nature. In this group the stalking reflects a desire for reconciliation, revenge, or a fluctuating mixture of both. This is common among domestic relationships and has resulted in several well-publicized murders.

2. The **Intimacy Seeker** desires a relationship with someone who has engaged their affection and who, they are convinced, already does, or will, reciprocate that love despite obvious evidence to the contrary; this is common among celebrities and are usually strangers to the stalker who believes they know and love.

3. The **Incompetent Suitor** also engages in stalking to establish a relationship. However, unlike the **Intimacy Seeker**, they are simply seeking a date or a sexual encounter. Their behaviour is driven by loneliness or lust, and targets strangers or acquaintances.

4. The **Resentful Stalker** sets out to frighten and distress the victim to exact revenge for an actual or supposed injury. **Resentful Stalkers** are differentiated from **Rejected Stalkers** in that the cause of their resentment does not lie in rejection from an intimate relationship. They feel as though they have been mistreated or that they are the victim of some form of injustice or humiliation.

5. The **Predatory Stalker** engages in pursuit behaviour to obtain sexual gratification. Stalking is foreplay; the real goal is sexual assault. The stalking may have a sadistic quality to it. For example, some predatory stalkers mess with their victim's minds by leaving subtle clues that they are being followed without revealing their identity.

Risk factors

The risks from a stalker should never be underestimated. There have been several cases where evidence of stalking existed and yet was not recognized nor acted on and resulted in a preventable murder being committed. It is for this reason it is important to recognize the difference between *harassment* and *stalking*. Misdiagnosing stalking as harassment can have fatal consequences and undermines the seriousness of the devastating consequences it has on the recipient.

It is regrettable that the police in the UK have a poor track record when recognizing and investigating stalking. In 2022, a super-complaint was submitted by the Suzy Lamplugh Trust, on behalf of the National Stalking Consortium, about the police response to stalking. In September 2024, His Majesty's Inspectorate of Constabulary and Fire and Rescue Services (HMICFRS) published their findings which accepted that "in too many cases the police response was not good enough and victims were being let down". If you believe you are being stalked, do not let the police persuade you that it is *just* harassment; where appropriate, request to speak to a more senior officer or seek the help of an advocate from one of the charities, such as the Suzy Lamplugh Trust.

If in any doubt, my website has an online assessment that helps you to recognize stalking, if you are unsure. The assessment can be found at: https://harassmentandstalker.scoreapp.com/

The risk factors that are specific to the relationship between the stalker and the recipient of their unwanted attention should be key elements of any stalking assessment, including:

- previous violence towards the recipient (during the stalking episode or before)
- threats or fantasies of harming the recipient
- delusional beliefs incorporating the recipient
- damage to the recipient's property
- behaviours that put them near the recipient, and/or
- breaching of any injunctions or orders.

These issues are relevant to the recipient but not necessarily to the wider community.

What to do if your clients are being stalked

1. Keep a record/diary of everything

Keeping records is hugely important, both to demonstrate what's going on and to keep a log. Because it's so difficult to define stalking, many agencies and professionals have such a hard time really trying to get their heads around what it is; your client's log of events and how they have made them feel can be invaluable. So always keep the evidence, keep everything possible, and if it's unpleasant give it someone else to keep.

Keep a record of how the events made them feel. How did they feel when the received a text or a phone call? Describe any changes they have made, such as increased security, changes to their phone number or moving home.

2. Don't keep it a secret

Being harassed or stalked is never the recipient's fault. They have done nothing wrong. Some stalkers will engage with their friends and family and in some cases have successfully persuaded them that their victim is going mad. Share what is happening with friends and family, and (where applicable) work colleagues. Ask them to keep a record of any contact they have or is made by the stalker. If you don't share what is happening, they won't know; let them in and let them help you.

3. Engage with a stalking advocate

Specialist services such as Defuse Global and the Suzy Lamplugh Trust provide advocates who will support you and your client to engage with the police. Suky Bhaker, CEO of the Suzy Lamplugh Trust and another guest on The Defuse Podcast said that when you engage with an advocate, the chances of a successful prosecution increase dramatically. However, I highly recommend engaging with an advocate even if you don't wish to prosecute.

4. Review the security

This does not need to be an expensive, highly technical procedure. Simple tasks such as changing the wi-fi and other passwords are useful exercises, especially if the stalker is an ex-partner or known to your client. If your client has recently misplaced keys, consider changing the locks. Invest in a doorbell camera; this prevents the door being opened to strangers and acts as a CCTV camera should someone approach the home. Consider reviewing their digital presence. This will, when done professionally, help to identify what private information is publicly available and help make them less vulnerable.

Dealing with the victims of stalking

Having worked with several people who were targeted and stalked, it's critical to recognize that they are all different, as are their experiences. However, there are some common traits that I believe are important to be mindful of.

The very experience of being targeted causes some to be paranoid and hypervigilant. This means that they may refer to feeling threatened when there is no apparent threat. The paranoia causes them to see, feel or experience a feeling of being unsafe. Stalking can take place in different environments, from within relationships, the workplace and from strangers.

It is recognized that, very often, their experiences and concerns are not taken seriously. It is not unusual for organizations to consider their reputations before the safety of the employee and seek to either reduce stalking behaviours to harassment or fail to recognize that their responsibilities and duty of care continues beyond the workplace, when employees are involved.

UK Policing was subject to a super-complaint,[30] which suggests there are deep-rooted systemic issues across police forces that are putting many victims at risk. I can give my experiences from both sides of the fence, having investigated stalking cases both as a police officer and as a private consultant. My experience tells me that policing continues to fail the victims of stalking by not recognizing the impact being stalked has to those targeted. All too often, the advice provided by police officers is inaccurate, misleading or dismissive.

Those targeted by a stalker will benefit from having an advocate who will help them to understand their legal rights and the current legislation, advise them to keep records of evidence or do so on their behalf, support them when they apply for safety orders against harassment, and keeping them updated on their court cases.

I often engage with the police, courts, lawyers and other professionals in the criminal system on their behalf and help them to make sense of what they are being told. I also provide emotional support and assistance by assessing risks, and creating plans for protection – an area that, in my experience, the police are very poor at doing. By acting as their advocate, I encourage them to get back to business as usual, while I manage the investigation and what often become stressful and confusing interactions with the criminal justice system.

Too often the engagement and communication from the police is inconsistent, and this can escalate the anxiety the victim experiences.

Summary

Many people experience unwanted attention. When that unwanted attention is from a person who has developed a fixation and is repeated, it can psychologically impact the person on the receiving end. In the UK, the law requires a 'course of conduct', which is two or more incidents, initially close together, for the offences of harassment and stalking to be committed. The difference between stalking and harassment is that stalkers are significantly more dangerous, and their behaviour has led to several murders.

Harassment is when they make the victim feel distressed, humiliated or threatened. The main goal of harassment is to persuade victims either not to do something they are entitled to or required to do, or to do something they are not obliged to do.

Stalking is a pattern or cluster of fixated and obsessive behaviours that are repeated, persistent and intrusive, and cause fear of violence or engender alarm and distress in the victim. Victims of stalking often change their own behaviour. There are five accepted types of stalkers, each caused by different emotions and targeted at different people.

The response from the criminal justice system is very often poor, inconsistent and the information provided inaccurate. The benefits of a victim having an advocate are significant and can be delivered by victim support services or specialist private providers. All victims should be encouraged to have an advocate.

Chapter 4

Communicated threats

Introduction

For many, the assumption is that the main channel of threats is via social media. However, this assumption is misleading. Increasingly, many of the threats you may face will be in the workplace. Research I conducted with Oxford University indicates a correlation between an economic decline, which we in the UK are experiencing at the time of writing, and an increase in workplace hostility and insider threats. This, for some, is compounded by a misogynist agenda, which has a direct impact on the type of threats that are made, who to and who by. Whatever your sex, this agenda is an important one to understand. The impact of being targeted or singled out is significant. Not all threats and abuse are physical in nature, but most have a deep psychological impact and can have a long-lasting effect on performance, mental health, judgement and decision-making.

In an age of social media and the internet, it is easy to become trapped in the illusion that those who communicate threats to you are the people you must be concerned about. There is an assumption that those people who make threats intend or are likely to cause physical violence. History and detailed research tell us that this is rarely the case. In this chapter, I will share the proven methodology that the most elite threat assessors use and that you can use to triage any threats that you are made aware of. This methodology is especially useful when the threat is communicated by an anonymous source, which often causes greater fear and anxiety.

Social media enables a perception of direct access to public figures. With that perception, there is an assumption that you communicate directly with the profile owner, which can cause critical issues. Some public figures respond and engage in a discussion, while others will have no engagement and employ a team to manage their online profiles. Many have commented on the hostility directed towards them, whether politicians, sports and entertainment stars, or business leaders. You may have experienced this yourself and will understand the associated anxiety and fear that happens when a threat is received.

While the world has changed, it was interesting that during the Brexit hostility, fewer than 13% of all the abuse reported by politicians emanated via social media. This is a surprisingly low figure, especially considering the volume of social media usage and the publicity it attracted. Much of the abuse received was communicated via telephone, written letters and email. The reason for this is that despite the presence of politicians online, due to the nature of their work, they still openly publish their phone numbers and parliamentary and constituency addresses, and any mail sent can be done so free of charge.

That said, communicated threats has been subject to significant research over the past 40 years, and the outcomes have been consistent.

In the early 1990s researchers found that far from there being any relationship between those who make threats and those who attack, the presence of a directly communicated threat may lower the risk that the threatener intends to 'pursue and encounter'.[31]

The US Secret Service Exceptional Case Study Project Report (see endnote 1) concluded as far back as 1997 that those who target public figures rarely directly communicate their intentions to their targets or to law enforcement. In his 2001 study, Dr Reid Meloy also concluded that 'most individuals who directly communicate a threat are not subsequently violent, and most individuals who do not directly communicate a threat are not subsequently violent'.[32] The research has since been replicated in mainland Europe and the UK, with the same results.

From these research studies, we can conclude that it is rare for an attacker to warn or directly threaten their intended target. Dr Reid Meloy, when discussing this as a guest on The Defuse Podcast (see endnote 2), suggested that the percentage of individuals who attack a public figure they have directly threatened is quite small, probably no more than 5%. It must be remembered that that is still 5% and, therefore, cannot be universally discounted (see endnote 23).

The intimacy factor

The 'Hunter and Howler' concept works well with public figures but less so in relationships where intimacy is or has been an issue. It is for this reason that domestic stalkers who threaten MUST be taken seriously. Research tells us that in these cases, those threatened have been found to be three times more likely to be physically attacked.[33] This fact is critical when managing risk.

When looked at from a less academic view, the question is: Why would someone warn you of an impending or intended attack? Why would they let you know what their plans are? The answer is that they wouldn't. Those individuals who make threats and abuse public figures are doing so to cause fear, anxiety, and intimidation. Threateners can be angry, disenfranchised people, but they are rarely dangerous.

Hunters and Howlers

One of the best analogies for this is the concept of 'Hunters and Howlers'. This concept was introduced by Calhoun and Weston when seeking to differentiate those who pose a threat from those who make them. The image on the front of their book is of two wolves… one howling and one not. The image beautifully encapsulates the theory. I visited the Negev desert in Israel some years ago. We were out for the night, and we could hear wolves howling during that time. I mentioned this to my fellow 'campers', who reassured me that it is fine to hear the wolves as they communicate. When they go quiet, you need to worry because then they are hunting!

Calhoun came up with the names for the concepts from two cases he dealt with. One was a person who happened to be a recreational hunter with a substantial collection of guns, who was charged by the Federal Government for possession of a large amount of cannabis. Without warning and driven by a sense of injustice, the Hunter in that person went to the courthouse and shot his way in, killing a court security officer in the process. He then killed himself.

The term *Howler* came from a federal prisoner who wrote horrific letters to a judge about the things they were going to do to him and his family. When challenged about their reason for writing the letters, the prisoner said they had nothing else to do. For them, it was just a hobby they drew pleasure from (see endnote 23).

You will no doubt have experienced the Howlers. They are the ones who communicate abuse and threats. The trolls.

Many of the politicians in Parliament were targeted by Howlers. However, because of misinformation by uneducated 'experts' who led them to believe these were a 'threat to democracy', fear spread like wildfire.

Howlers can be very scary. Their intention is to draw attention to themselves. They want to frighten people, but they don't intend to do these terrible things they write about in their communications. So Howlers are rarely violent, but they still pose a problem. Howlers must still be managed, so the policy of ignoring them completely or blocking them can be a mistake. A common policy is to use technology to block any messages with certain, usually offensive, keywords contained in the message. This can be a dangerous strategy, as the messages may, in fact, provide evidence of escalation. A threat may be building in the background, to which you are oblivious.

Case Study

A client reported a female for harassment. Just before I was due to leave the office to conduct the necessary enquiries, I took a phone call from the client, who, in a sudden 'flash of inspiration', remembered that contrary to what he had previously said, he did know the female; he'd had a one-night stand with her at a hotel. This admission changed the entire risk profile of the investigation. The risk profile was increased due to the intimate relationship. The harassment was also seen differently, as the person contacting the client was aggrieved by the client's behaviour. A response to the person was drafted, causing all contact to end.

Some threats are genuine and must be taken seriously. The question then is: How do you know which threats to treat seriously? This is obviously a key question. It matters, because even if the threat isn't followed through, as a public figure you will want to know when to add to your security, what to add and what will make a difference.

If we accept the fact that according to research and expertise, very few who make a direct threat pose a threat, the obvious next question is: How do I identify a real threat?

During my dissertation for my MSc in Security Management, I explored this question. I wanted to know, as an operational professional, what I should look for.

I researched all attacks or planned attacks on British MPs since 2000. There were a few trends, but the one that stood out was that none of those attacked or subject to a planned attack had been threatened by their attacker. This, therefore, reinforced the 'Hunter and Howler' theory as described previously. The other trends that were highlighted were behavioural.

Within the world of threat management, there is a sub-niche called 'behavioural threat management'. This is the sub-niche that I focus on. The premise is, to coin a phrase, 'actions speak louder than words'. A person's behaviours will determine whether they pose a threat. It is worth adding that communicating is just one of many behaviours to be considered.

In the next couple of chapters, I will delve deeper into the specific behaviours that have been identified as the proximal indicators.

It is very easy, especially in the age of the internet and social media, to make a threat or abuse someone. There is a lot of research about why people feel more liberated to say on the internet what they wouldn't say in person, but even without the academic rigour, most can imagine the consequences of saying in public what is said on the internet: a likely punch on the nose!

In general terms this book is about intended or targeted attacks; rather, the spontaneous emotive, affective violence which was discussed earlier in the book. With that in mind it is reasonable to ask why would someone who is intending to attack want to broadcast their intentions, although interestingly, many do. They just don't do it directly. To be clear, I am not referring to the professional hitman (or hitwoman), but to a problematic individual, fixated person or lone actor.

Whenever we hear of an attack in the news, we will be introduced to a witness who, with the benefit of hindsight, was aware of a change in behaviour or leaked intention on behalf of the attacker, and yet they failed to either recognize the importance of those signs at the time or not know whom to tell. Under-reporting of problem individuals to the authorities is a significant vulnerability. This is a recurring pattern seen in attacks on educational facilities, shopping malls and workplaces.

The origin of most threat assessments is the identification phase. A problem or problem person has been identified. The challenge is that unless a report is made by someone who has experienced or witnessed a behaviour of concern, the 'identification' phase never happens.

You may employ the most sophisticated threat assessment team going. However, unless others in the organization, such as the HR, administrative, secretaries and other professionals – including those involved in logistics and transport, gardeners, and front-line security – know what they are looking for, your threat assessment team will be under-employed.

Calhoun and Weston's most recent research seeks to fill that gap. Titled 'Imagining the Unimaginable', they have introduced a pre-identification strategy which they have called 'Detect, Report, Act'.[34]

This important new research hypothesizes that relying on trained threat assessors is problematic. However, when we train the other professionals mentioned earlier to adopt an 'All Threat – All Reporting' mindset, it is more likely that a problematic person or situation is identified. Calhoun and Weston found that while many of us will report an incident when we have been personally threatened, we are less likely to recognize behaviours of concern as being 'indicative' of potential violence and hence won't report them. Training is, therefore, essential.

The earlier a threat assessment professional can identify a person of concern, the better. This identification also enables early elimination of them being a possible attacker. That said, untrained threat assessors are equally unlikely to 'imagine the unimaginable', and so it is important that any assumptions about the level of proper training security and others in the protective environment are confirmed.

Reporting criteria

As Calhoun and Weston state (see endnote 35), the following are, in broad terms, behaviours that should be reported to either a designated professional or the authorities:

- all threats of physical harm
- any violence, including criminal damage
- any problematic terminations, suspensions, or other disciplinary outcomes
- any inappropriate behaviour
- any expressions of personal loss, injustice, or a desire for revenge
- any inappropriate reference to weapons or inflicting harm, death, suicide, or violence
- any suggestion of delusional beliefs or paranoia
- any indication of research and planning, surveillance, or unusual enquiries into security practices
- any indication of 'final acts' such as disposing of property, saying goodbye, last rights, or justification of violence, and
- testing of security, perimeters, or systems.

This is not an exhaustive list, and where you are unsure, always seek professional advice.

It is important when reviewing systems that a proper and well-published line of reporting is established. For individuals, this might simply be reporting matters to the police. However, be mindful that most UK police officers are not trained in threat management and so may not immediately recognize the signs of escalation.

For organizations, this will require a more formal process. We know from the statistics quoted in Chapter 5 (Workplace violence) that many people fail to report their concerns because they simply don't know what to report and who to report their concerns to. Equally, responding promptly and engaging with an identified complainant is key. It is key that whenever trained staff leave, they are replaced by others equally properly trained. These staff must know what to do with the reported information. This may be reporting concerns to the police or, where appropriate, to a multi-disciplined internal team. All too often, concerns are left unreported until the end of the week, and then suddenly, a flurry of reports is made just before staff leave for the weekend. Clear protocols must be agreed upon and followed.

Hate crime

Any crime can be prosecuted as a hate crime if the offender has demonstrated hostility based on race, religion, disability, sexual orientation or transgender identity, or if they have been motivated by such hostility.[35]

When investigating any situation where hate crimes are believed to have been involved, it is essential to recognize the critical importance of prioritizing victim security concerns. Where possible, addressing the unique fears, distress and potential for reprisal and escalating violence experienced by victims is an important consideration. It is crucial to acknowledge the extensive negative impact of these crimes on those impacted, emphasizing the need to support victims and their families.[36]

While misogyny is not recognized as a hate crime per se, it is an important subject. Indeed, it is as relevant for men as it is for women, and I believe it should be treated with the same sensitivity and seriousness as other hate crimes.

To overcome misogyny, men must understand the issue as well as women and be willing to change. As a man, consider this from the perspective of your mother, your female partner, sister, daughter or niece. As a woman... well, you will know this subject only too well.

One of the first things that struck me when setting up and running the investigative team in Parliament was the difference in abuse and threats the female politicians received from those the men received.

The targeting of female politicians was significant. This was perhaps magnified because of the murder of Jo Cox MP that precipitated me setting up the team.[37]

The abuse received by women is far more personal, making references to every perceived flaw in their looks, dress sense, apparent sexuality and sexual preference. The threats are routinely sexually violent in their nature.

Most of the individuals sending these abusive and threatening messages were men. Despite what much of the research says, mental health wasn't the issue; inadequacy was. My assessment of many of these men, based on their lifestyles and excuses to some degree, was that they felt threatened by successful, influential and powerful women. These female politicians had everything they didn't. The impact of these appalling communications was significant. It was very clear the politicians were being targeted because they were women, and in my professional opinion, that meant they should be treated as hate crimes. They were not.

While some dismiss the 'Me too' movement as irrelevance, it is far too serious, and the issues too routed to be treated so lightly. The sad fact is that 80% of victims of stalking are women. Suky Bhaker from the Suzy Lamplugh Trust was a guest on The Defuse Podcast and stated that 88% of respondents surveyed by the Trust had experienced unwanted violent, aggressive or sexual behaviours on UK public transport in the last five years, and 90% of them had experienced unwanted behaviours, at least once in their lifetime.

This is by no means a UK-centric issue. In her book *I Hate Men*, French author Pauline Harmange stated that 90% of people who received death threats from their partners were women, while 86% of those murdered by a current or former partner were women.[38] Interestingly, the book was subjected to a censorship attempt by France's Ministry of Gender Equality in 2020.

The abduction and murder of Sarah Everard by a police officer rightly shocked the nation.[39] This was further compounded by the conviction of a colleague of Sarah's killer as a serial rapist.[40] Trust in the police plummeted. Whereby, once, women would feel safe calling upon a male police officer to help them, this is no longer the case.

This has seen the emergence of schemes such as 'Ask for Angela'. The safety initiative 'Ask for Angela'[41] was rolled out to licensed venues such as bars and clubs. Women who felt unsafe, vulnerable or threatened could discretely approach staff and ask them for 'Angela'. This indicates to staff that the asker requires help with their situation, and a trained staff member will then look to support and assist them.

Whether women and girls are feeling less safe is no longer up for debate. It has been suggested that the stress resulting from economic downturn has caused an increase in male feelings of dominance being threatened.[42] This may result in an increase in sexual harassment and violence, and interestingly whereas the vast majority of victims are women, periods of economic downturn are also accompanied by an increase of complaints by men, even though routinely men are still paid more than women in the same role, and many would argue still have better opportunities for advancement.

The challenge is that even men in inferior social and economic roles sense they can harass women, which indicates an example of male feelings of dominance. It is this dominance that is the problem.

For some, this is a communication issue. When at work, how do women feel about leaving the building late at night? Do they have to walk to the station or to a car park? Have you discussed these issues with colleagues or clients?

Walking down a street or leaving a venue in the dark is a very different experience for men and women. For many women this activity requires a risk assessment. The challenge for many men, conscious how their presence may be misconstrued or not, is knowing how to react when they think a woman is in distress.

Statistics from surveys completed by L'Oréal Paris and IPSOS[43] between 2019 and 2021 revealed:

- 80% of women in the UK have reported experiencing harassment in public spaces
- 75% of UK harassment victims said no one helped
- 93% of UK women and 90% of UK men believe there is lack of training on how to intervene
- 86% of UK witnesses who have intervened reported that their action improved the situation
- 86% of UK respondents say they did not intervene because they do not know what to do.

The Suzy Lamplugh Trust has developed 'Harassment Bystander Training' to increase awareness of harassment and empowering everyone to help defuse situations, discourage harassers and support victims.

Physical, reputational and psychological harm

Targeted attacks and threats are often seen in the context of physical threats. However, increasingly reputational threats are of concern and, with that, the increased psychological impact of being targeted. In this section, we will discuss these issues.

Many of the case studies used when referring to targeted violence are seen from the perspective of those who have been physically attacked. This is understandable, as the impact is visible and often catastrophic. When I first entered Parliament to investigate the threats and abuse UK politicians were receiving, my focus was on the physical threats and whether they contravened the law. Often, the conversation with those targeted would involve other areas of concern.

One of the most significant by-products of being targeted is the emotional and psychological cost. It quickly became apparent to me that some of those targeted were reporting other offences and concerns that were unrelated or non-existent. They had become paranoid and hypervigilant, looking for and finding threats everywhere, and making assumptions and connections where none existed.

There are several elements to consider in understanding the psychological impact.

From a mental health perspective, there is a range of emotions that your clients may have experienced. Some are in complete denial, refusing to see the signs right before them. This is especially relevant when they know the person targeting them. I have witnessed others who have become suicidal and feeling unable to cope. Yet others have become depressed, feeling guilty as if they had done something to encourage unwanted attention. Then there are those who experienced increased alcohol consumption and lack of sleep, with constant rumination, fear and anxiety every time they receive an email, a call, or a message that it will be from the person of concern. These emotions become exhausting, along with the impact of decision-making, lack of trust and insecurity.

Because of the exhausting emotions described, it is not unusual to then experience physical effects such as lack of focus, fatigue, being increasingly isolated, loss of sexual appetite, break up of relationships or snapping at colleagues, dizziness, weight gain, heart palpitations and anxiety. To counter this, additional coffee, drugs or alcohol are often consumed, which can then cause other negative emotions.[44]

These physical effects can then impact performance, which may cause their decision-making to be impaired or create an inability to make decisions and raise their concerns about the increasing costs of additional security needs.

During the Brexit debates, it was common for a politician to be inundated with threats, abuse, intimidation and being called a traitor, causing them to question how they were going to vote. Because their voting record was published, they knew that if they voted a certain way, the likelihood of abuse and threats would increase.

The recent UK Government study referred to in endnote 45 identified that even those who feel resilient to being trolled and targeted may, in fact, change their behaviours when they witness others being targeted.

One client was a hugely successful and resilient person. Their journey to success had been long and hard-fought, and initially they were dismissive of being trolled and targeted online. That changed when they began to receive letters and parcels through the post, demonstrating that the person of concern knew where they lived. That was the straw that broke the camel's back.

Another client chose to remove their profile from social media. This wasn't a decision that was easily made. They had spent years building their network, had monetized that network, and knew that by leaving their income, further opportunities would take a significant hit.

A further concern is the reputational harm that is caused.

Case Study

In 2016, Wikileaks published emails from Hilary Clinton's campaign chairman, John Podesta. One email included a reference to James Alefantis, who is the owner of Comet Ping Pong, a Washington-based pizza restaurant. He had previously raised money for the Democratic party and supported Obama and Clinton. From this, an entirely fictional story was concocted about a paedophile sex ring involving prominent politicians and political donors from pictures of children and modern art on his restaurant walls. These stories were published on 4Chan, an extreme right-wing message board that was soon picked up by Trump supporters and spread via mainstream media outlets.

Alefantis, along with his employees and others, started getting threatening messages, causing him to lock his Instagram account. This fake story, called 'Pizzagate', created an entire conspiracy, with some suggesting Clinton should be prosecuted. One man armed with a gun turned up outside the restaurant and opened fire, suggesting he was 'investigating' the matter.[45]

We will perhaps never know the true impact on Clinton's election hopes. However, it was part of a wider online strategy to discredit her.

The important lesson is that not all targeted attacks are physical attempts to kill.

Summary

Not all threats are equal. Identifying and prioritizing which threats require immediate attention should be a critical skill of any security professional. Social media has enabled threats to be communicated to contacts and strangers instantly and often anonymously, causing fear and anxiety. It has also caused security professionals and law enforcement to respond to each threat as if genuine. This has wasted resources and, in many cases, encouraged perpetrators to communicate further threats. While all threats should be reviewed, in general terms, and regarding threats made to strangers, those who make a threat rarely pose one. These perpetrators are called Howlers, and their intentions are to intimidate and to spread anxiety and fear from afar. They rarely go on to attack. Conversely, when the recipient and the perpetrator are or have been in an intimate relationship, all threats must be taken seriously and assumed to be genuine until proven otherwise.

Chapter 5

Work-related violence

Introduction

The term *workplace violence* often conjures up images of mass shootings committed by deranged former employees armed with assault rifles. The major challenge with the term is the word *violence*. While physical violence may occur in the extreme, incidents of minor assaults, bullying, intimidation, harassment and stalking, together with domestic violence, are far more likely and more common than many realize. In this section, I will provide definitions and explanations of what the term means, the causes and some of the processes that help to manage, if not quite eliminate, the issues.

Definition

There are various approved descriptions of *workplace violence*, which include:

> A spectrum of behaviours, including overt acts of violence, threats and other conduct, that generates a reasonable concern for the safety from violence, where a nexus exists between the behaviour and the physical safety of employees and other (such as customers, clients and business associates) on-site or off-site when related to the organisation.[46]

The US FBI defined it as 'any action that may threaten the safety of an employee, impact an employee's physical, or psychological wellbeing or cause damage to company property'.[47]

Causes

Broadly speaking, the sources or causes of workplace violence fall into four categories.

1. **Criminal intent:** acts of violence by those who enter the workplace to commit a crime, such as robbery. These can also include current or former employees who come to work with that intent and may be seen as insiders.
2. **Customer/client:** acts of violence directed at employees by anyone who comes under the mantle of being a customer, including an inmate, student, patient or client.
3. **Employee:** acts of violence in the workplace directed at another employee, supervisor or manager by a current or former employee.
4. **Personal:** acts that are directed at an employee in the workplace by a person connected to the employee but not the employer.

Some studies include a further category to incorporate terrorism.

5. **Terrorism:** where the organization or workplace is subjected to a targeted or random attack intended to cause fatalities or economic or reputational harm.[48]

Personally, I believe the 'Terrorism' category falls under 'Criminal intent' (number 1 in the list) and may have been added to enable greater resources to be secured to prevent or tackle such issues.

I recently conducted a research project with Oxford University to consider whether there was a correlation between an economic decline and increased workplace violence and insider threats. Our research concluded that there is a correlation and that, because of this, an increase is to be expected.[49] The research found that employees feel left behind and their concerns unheard, and this sense of injustice drives some towards a more hostile perspective.

It has been reported by a 2016 UK Trade Union Congress survey that more than 60% of women have reported being sexually harassed at work.[50] Further evidence of the scale of the problem suggests that 29% of people have been victims of workplace bullying in the UK. That's nearly 3 in every 10 workers, equating to 9.1 million of the UK workforces.[51] To compound the issue, over 90% of employees didn't report their concerns to the employer as they believed they failed to deal with reports properly.[52]

While employees, managers and others are equally vulnerable to such attacks, this book focuses on business leaders rather than employees.

The Ontic Centre for Protective Intelligence,[53] an international hub for current and past security trends, identified a worrying fact when considering CEOs: 58% of them received physical threats after taking position on racial and/or political issue. What's more, some 40% of CEOs received physical threats because they had NOT taken a position on racial and/or political issues. In essence, if you are protecting a CEO there is strong likelihood they will receive threats.

A further element for this is that C-Suite executives (in other words, CEOs, CFOs, COOs and CIOs) repeatedly demonstrate that they underestimate how much their employees are struggling with their wellbeing. Our research found that only 56% believe their executive's care. In contrast, 91% of the C-Suite executives believe that workers feel their leader's care. (You can read more on this in endnote 50.) This is compounded by the fact that only 47% of workers believe their executives understand how difficult the COVID-19 Pandemic was for them, while 90% of those C-Suite executives claim they do understand.

It is this disparity that creates risks for the C-Suite, with a decline in mental health, rising cost of living expenses and a lack of opportunities at work damaging the sense of belonging, loyalty and, for some, perspective. At the time of writing, the UK is still experiencing ongoing industrial actions in several different industries.

This is experienced when, following an incident, colleagues will often express that the perpetrator 'was a ticking time bomb' or how they just 'snapped', with others suggesting that 'there was always something odd about them' and 'I worried this would happen'.

As I have explained in Chapter 4, while some do snap (affective violence), even those who do, do so for a reason. The behaviours of concern were witnessed and known by many, but no one knew what they meant, who to report them to, or were too concerned by various policies that they may fall foul of to say anything.

Even when these concerns are reported, while many organizations believe they have the appropriate resources to manage any outbursts of workplace violence, this tends not to be the case, with very little proper behavioural threat management training or expertise existing.[54]

In Chapter 2 we discussed grievances, and many, if not most, of the workplace violence incidents are driven by a grievance. Very often the C-Suite are targeted, because they are the representatives of an organization. To prevent incidents of workplace violence and insider threats, early identification of problematic people is essential.

Case Study

The CEO of a global brand had been subject to targeted threats by a former employee who had left the organization some years previously. The former employee considered that, in hindsight, he had been treated unfairly, which caused them to leave. The blame, as far as he was concerned, sat with the CEO, despite the fact they were new. The CEO, whose phone number had (for some reason) been published, began to receive messages from an unknown number. The messages became increasingly hostile, referring to the CEO's family and home. An image of the CEO's home was sent with the clear inference, 'I know where you live'.

The messages escalated to making direct threats to the safety of the CEO's family if the concerns were not listened to. This understandably caused significant anxiety and fear for the CEO and their family, with additional security being deployed.

An online meeting was agreed, and the former employee began the meeting with several false accusations of his treatment and why he felt he should be compensated. The former employee threatened to harm the company's reputation and 'expose' his treatment.

Our investigation identified that the former employee was suffering from a narcissistic personality disorder and had made similar threats to other former employers. His threats were sent to intimidate and cause fear, although he lacked the capability to carry them out. In this case, we advised sending a formal letter to the former employee to lay out the conditions of his termination and justification. The letter instructed the former employee that there would be no further engagement between them, and should he feel further aggrieved, he was advised to continue his complaints via legal means.

The contact from the former employee stopped.

Bullying and harassment

Bullying and harassment are behaviours that make someone feel intimidated or offended. In the UK, harassment at work is unlawful under the Equality Act 2010 as well as being a criminal offence, a fact often overlooked. Typical behaviours can include:

- unwanted physical contact
- unwelcome comments about someone's age, dress, appearance, race or marital status
- jokes at personal expense, offensive language, gossip, slander, sectarian songs and letters, often referred to as banter
- isolation or non-cooperation and exclusion from social activities
- coercion for sexual favours – sexual harassment
- pressure to participate in political/religious groups
- personal intrusion from pestering, spying and stalking
- persistent unwarranted criticism
- personal insults.

Sexual harassment

Employers and business leaders need to be more proactive ahead to protect employees from sexual harassment. From October 2024, employers will need to comply with a legal duty to take 'reasonable steps' aiming to prevent sexual harassment of employees. This follows the passing of the Worker Protection (Amendment of Equality Act 2010) Act 2023.

Under the Act, employment tribunals will have the power to increase compensation by up to 25% if it finds that an employer has breached this duty. Too many companies are woefully ill-prepared for the changes coming down the line.

The key is to be proactive right now. Employers who delay may find themselves extremely vulnerable when the new law comes in.

Despite laws against such behaviour, the statistics indicate more needs to be done to address and prevent these incidents.

Employers need to prioritize preventing sexual harassment at work by taking proactive steps. The new legislation emphasizes the importance of consistently reviewing and updating harassment policies. It will also require employers to conduct frequent training sessions, and handle complaints seriously.

At the same time, it's crucial for employers to take consistent action beyond policies and training to foster a safe and inclusive workplace. Regular workplace assessments are essential to ensure the effectiveness of existing measures. Training that focuses on behavioural indicators rather than conflict management can be useful in such nuanced issues.

Apart from the human response and the obvious duty of care, failing to be proactive may result in many other problems. These can include legal consequences like lawsuits and compensation claims, reputational damage, reduced employee morale, and increased turnover and decreased productivity from employees.

Here are eight steps employers should implement to protect employees.

1. **Have clear policies:** Develop and communicate clear policies on sexual harassment.
2. **Invest in training:** Introduce new regular training for all employees on recognizing and preventing harassment.
3. **Ensure you have reporting mechanisms:** Establish straightforward procedures for reporting harassment.
4. **Conduct prompt investigations:** Investigate all complaints promptly and thoroughly, and be mindful of incidents where criminal offences may have been committed.
5. **Guarantee confidentiality:** Ensure that complaints are handled confidentially.
6. **Make sure you offer non-retaliation:** Protect complainants from retaliation.
7. **Take appropriate actions:** Take disciplinary action against perpetrators when necessary.
8. **Offer support for victims:** Provide access to counselling and support services.

Insider threats

Insider threat is not a new subject, albeit one that is more readily discussed. Perhaps the earliest case can be traced back to biblical times, when according to Christianity, Judas betrayed Jesus Christ to the Romans. For many, the term *Judas* signifies one who cannot be trusted and betrays the trust given to them. In more recent times, there have been several equally high-profile cases of such betrayal; often seen as an IT issue, it remains a human-centric issue. This section will define what an insider threat is, establish some of the behavioural issues that may help detect it and provide guidance to protect against it.

Rarely a day goes by when the term *insider threat* isn't mentioned in the news. Enter the term into a search engine and you'll receive around 61,400,000 results. For the basis of this topic, I think a definition is the best place to start. What is an insider threat? Depending on whom you choose to listen to, you will receive several different responses, with one study eliciting 42 different definitions.[55] The definition I use is:

> An insider threat is an individual who is either an employee, contractor or vendor who has access to the organisation's information, material, people and facilities who, based on that access has the potential to harm the organization due to malice, complacency or ignorance. Insider threat examples include data exfiltration, fraud, sabotage, workplace violence or espionage.[56]

To counter such threats, you will require a process that identifies, assesses, mitigates and deters anyone, whether they are malicious, complacent or ignorant, from causing you harm.

People have different reasons and motivations for becoming an insider threat, but what is clear is that the vast majority don't join an organization with premeditated intent. Research by the National Protective Security Authority (NPSA), the UK Government's National Technical Authority for physical and personnel protective security, found that only 6% of those they studied resulted from deliberate infiltration.[57]

The study by the NPSA did identify some interesting trends, which may prove helpful. Mindful that their research is focused on critical national infrastructure they identified that the primary motivation for those conducting an insider threat was:

- financial gain (47% of cases)
- ideology (20% of cases)
- desire for recognition (14% of cases)
- loyalty to friends/family/country (14% of cases)
- revenge (6% of cases).

One of the usual methods employed is pre-employment vetting or due diligence checks or investigations. These are carried out with a huge variant in complexity and effectiveness. Many see them as a tick-box requirement and an expense they'd rather do without. They are a legal requirement for others, especially those within government or high-risk environments. No matter what the level of complexity, they all fail.

The key to success in conducting due diligence is to instil a process that looks at behavioural changes, is repeated during the employee's time with the organization, is manually completed, and is far from being a tick-box exercise that investigates the individual.

While this may appear to be an expense many can do without, and while research on the cost of an insider threat varies, what they all agree on is that any attack is a hugely expensive incident and far outshines the cost of preventative measures.

Melissa Muir, a hugely experienced HR and threat assessment specialist, shared on our podcast (see endnote 23) that she introduced proactive due diligence, which was conducted prior to a candidate being interviewed. This enabled insight into candidates and facilitated a better interview while allowing any unsuitable candidates to be weeded out at an early stage. This, coupled with the fact that insider threats have increased by 50% in recent years, means that the subject must be taken seriously.[58]

It would be hard to imagine anyone being scrutinized more than Edward Snowdon, an IT contractor to the US Intelligence Agencies, and yet he went on to become one of history's most significant insider threats.[59] There have been a number of such insider threats from intelligence agencies across the globe, from different ideological perspectives, so again his act of treachery is not new.

On a more 'mundane' scale, Jessica Harper, Head of Fraud and Security for digital banking at Lloyd's Bank received a five-year prison sentence for her £2.4 million fraud, having submitted false invoices to claim payments between 2007 and 2011.[60]

The problem with pre-employment checks, vetting and due diligence is that all they really provide is a snapshot in time. They don't predict what will happen in the future, nor do they get behind the person to understand their personality, and nor in most cases do they identify risky lifestyle choices. Even with the most intrusive investigation, people and their circumstances change.

When considering the NPSA statistics on the primary motivation, financial gain is the number 1 reason. That motivation may be driven by pure greed or because of a costly divorce, the cost of living crisis, an addiction problem, a sick child or any number of reasons. In the increasingly challenging economic conditions currently being experienced by many, disgruntled employees who once may have left and sought a different job are staying put in fear of not being able to find a new position. Those disgruntled employees pose a huge risk to your organization.

A successful insider threat can have significant, if not catastrophic, consequences for any organization. An attack can be expensive to investigate and fix, and impact the share price and the safety of employees and customers, with many choosing to move to a competitor without understanding or caring about the facts.

Insider threats are not purely about hacking and malware; these threats are also about identity theft, CEO and executive fraud, often known as *whaling*, which involves impersonating a senior figure (usually the Chief Executive Officer) with subsequent requests for funds transfers. The attack can feature company email signatures, real names and even accurately spoofed email addresses. The issue with this type of fraud is simple: they look as realistic as possible and have a high chance of success.

Log on to LinkedIn any day, and you will see hundreds of unsuspecting victims sharing their news that they have secured a new position or been promoted. That is manna from heaven for those seeking to target individuals or their company. These people signal that they are unfamiliar with their new company's policies or processes and are likelier to open an email or link, especially when an urgency to respond is included.

If we take the perspective of an insider threat more likely to be a current employee, how then can you identify who they are?

In line with earlier advice I provided, there are two key aspects that must be in place to encourage reporting of any behaviours of concern.

First, there must be an environment of confidentiality. If a person feels there might be consequences for reporting behaviour of concern, they are unlikely to do so.[61]

Second, as described earlier, there needs to be a clear understanding of who to report concerns to and, equally, that where they report their concerns also knows what to do with them (refer to endnote 35 for more detail).

The key behaviours of concern are very often obvious to those involved with the person of concern; however, they are often not reported until an incident has occurred. (Take another look at endnote 62.)

The behaviours of concern include:

- copying and/or removing large quantities of data
- accessing data beyond their role
- ignoring rules such as opening links or downloading emails they shouldn't
- accessing areas that are beyond their clearance or need
- lateness or poor discipline
- poor performance or attitude
- attending the place of work out of hours or on days off
- becoming more vocal and critical of the organization.

Investigations

As highlighted in this chapter, one the issues with investigating toxic workplace behaviours is the lack of reporting. When investigating toxic behaviours, be they domestic violence, sexual abuse and assaults or workplace violence, trust is a key issue. It is rare for a person to report on the first occasion that they have been victimized, and in fact they very often won't report until they have been targeted on several occasions. Another factor is that they are unlikely to share with you all the details, or the details of the most serious incidents at first. It is quite usual for them to drip feed allegations, to see what the response is.

Are they believed? What is the response? Can they trust you/the organization to keep what they have shared confidential? Is the investigation conducted properly and fairly? Have you done what you said you would? If the answer is yes, trust may then be built, and they then may provide further details.

The very best way to investigate workplace issues is as part of a multi-disciplined team, usually involving representatives from human resources, legal, security and employee groups such as a union. The benefit of this structure is the likelihood of being fully informed, having access to different experts and ensuring that all parties are represented.

Multi-discipline teams such as these are more prominent is US-based organizations, and from July 2024, virtually every employer in California will be required to implement a comprehensive workplace violence prevention plan.[62] It is likely that this practice may be mirrored outside of California, and there is a growing demand for similar processes in the UK and elsewhere.

In my view, this is a positive step as everyone should feel safe in everyday life, and that should include while at work.

Summary

In this chapter, you will have learned about how threats and targeted violence impact the workforce. Despite having significant legislation such as the Health and safety Act and the Worker Protection Act 2023, some people still don't feel safe at work. The threats they experience may be classed as harassment, bullying or discrimination. A recent concern for many is the targeted attacks that occur in the workplace and at educational facilities. What is important is to recognize that the theories and methodologies discussed in this and previous chapters are also relevant at work.

Not all threats at work emanate from the workplace; some are from external sources such as unhappy customers, and partners and associates of employees who are engaged in some form of dispute which they bring to the workplace, as that is where they know their adversary will be.

A white paper that we published at Defuse evidenced the challenges that employers are increasingly facing in the workplace, and the financial, reputational, psychological and physical repercussions experienced when they fail to properly manage these issues. Whether you are an employer or work for an organization that employs others, the threat from your colleagues, co-workers, contractors and others is significant. Whatever the circumstances, having clear, confidential processes will encourage the reporting of behaviours of concern.

When an employee has been subjected to toxic or threatening behaviours, they may not immediately report their concerns and, when they do, they may not share all the details. Employees seek trust before they feel comfortable reporting their concerns.

The most effective response to toxic workplace behaviour is the create a multi-disciplined team, which ensures that those investigating have the broadest picture and can make decisions that support all parties involved.

Chapter 6

Threat escalation

Introduction

W hen a person's behaviour towards you is problematic, it is helpful to understand what to look out for and how to ascertain whether their behaviour is escalating. Threat management is not a static practice, but one where a person's concerning behaviour should be subject to constant evaluation to ascertain whether they are escalating or not.

The pathway to intended or targeted violence

Earlier in this book, I introduced the concept of there being two types of violence: the emotionally reactive type, and the slow burn type, which is calculated as the intended or predatory type. This chapter very specifically relates to intended or targeted violence, which follows a process that often includes planning and preparation.

One of the key models that has proved effective when identifying and assessing threats is known as 'The Pathway to Intended or Targeted Violence'. The US Secret Service study published in 1999 identified that the attackers they had studied followed distinct processes.[63] This process is witnessed in stalkers, activists, lone actor terrorists, school shooters and even nation-states. (Refer back to the Online Bodyguard podcast in endnote 23.)

While many might assume that the perpetrators of mass attacks must be stereotypical madmen flipping and running amok shooting widely, this image is far from accurate. Even those suffering from mental illness or personality disorders have been seen to follow a perfectly rational pattern of behaviour. Very few of these individuals are delusional during the attack.

This process was developed into a model known as 'The Pathway to Intended Violence' by my good friend Ted Calhoun and his colleague Steve Weston in their 2016 publication (see Figure 6.1).[64]

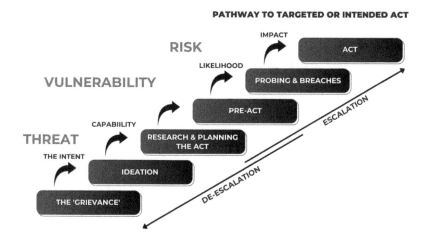

Figure 6.1: The Pathway to Intended Violence

The first step on this journey towards intended violence is the formation of a grievance. When someone decides they are unable to resolve their 'grievance' through peaceful means, they decide that violence might be their only option. This is when they move up a step to 'violent ideation'. This is a critical step, referred to by Calhoun as 'crossing the line' (again, refer back to endnote 23). A feeling of superiority or pretentiousness and a need for recognition can be a significant factor in this decision.[65]

This can be seen when activists decide that peaceful protests are not achieving their aims, and so move on to causing criminal damage and the destruction of property. Their perceived superiority causes them to feel that they know better than everyone else, as if they are more intelligent or their views more important.

In May 2010, Roshonara Choudhry, a 21-year-old British former student and an Islamist extremist, attempted to kill her local Member of Parliament, Stephen Timms MP.[66] She had developed a grievance online by secretly listening to extremist preachers when her family thought she was studying. Her decision to move to violent ideation was formed when she heard one of the preachers say that 'even women' had a duty to fight.[67] Before this, she told police, she believed only men were obligated to violent Jihad.[68]

The 'research and planning' step is next. Depending on the intended target, this can be very quick or can take months or even years. In a domestic violence scenario, you don't see a lot of research behaviour because the subject already knows where the partner works, what their routines are during the day and where they are most exposed. However, with a public figure where the subject doesn't know as much about the target, you see distinct behaviours. They are exploring how best to attack the subject of their obsession. Once upon a time, this would have involved a great deal of physical research or hostile reconnaissance. Much of the information sought can now be found via the internet and online maps.

Once they have completed their research, they then develop a plan of what they're going to do and how they are going to do it.

Having developed the intent and capability, the threat is formed.

The next step is the 'preparation or pre-attack phase' and where the vulnerabilities of the target are finalized.

This is where the person of concern will seek to acquire a weapon, access to the site or premises, identify where to conduct the attack, and plan the route. For more intricate plans, it will be where they seek to acquire what they need for the attack or begin any training they believe they require.

In the case of Anders Breivik, the right-wing extremist who attacked and killed students in Norway, this was a slow process. It began with him recognizing that he required significant funds, and he spent four years saving the money he required. A year before he conducted the attack he began preparing for it. He buried body armour in a forest and travelled to Prague to buy the weapons he wanted. When that trip failed, he completed the required Norwegian Government firearms training and then purchased the weapons he wanted. He had joined a pistol club five years before the attack to facilitate this.[69]

It is during this phase that opportunities to discover the person of concern can appear. Manifestos are written or recorded, and should the person of concern not plan to survive the attack, end-of-life behaviours can be witnessed (see endnote 66). Roshonara Choudhry closed her bank accounts, paid off her student loans, acquired the knives she intended to use, and dropped out of university.

During this phase, the final opportunities to thwart the attack often exist.

If a planned attack is identified, it is crucial to counter that plan as soon as possible. This may include moving the target, changing plans, adding layers of security, and reporting concerns to them if law enforcement has yet to be informed.

The next step up is the 'probing and breach' phase. This is when an attack may be initiated. This may be when the person of concern tests the security to see how they respond and what they do. They are looking for vulnerabilities. In 1994, Paul Hill decided to attack an abortion clinic in the USA.[70] During this phase of his plan, he conducted a drive past to double-check whether any additional security was present. As he drove past, a police vehicle crossed from the opposite direction. This startled him, so he continued driving. He then parked up, took his shotgun, walked back to the clinic and initiated his attack. This was a divergence from his original plan.[71]

There have been several cases where the subject gets close to the target and changes his or her mind. Something may go wrong; they get spooked or just back away. This may be the last opportunity to stop any attack.

If an opportunity arises, this phase can quickly escalate to the 'attack' phase. The last step is the actual attack. Once the attack occurs, the need for threat management is no longer necessary, and the protective security measures have failed.

The object of threat management is to divert persons of concern off this pathway to intended violence before they get to attack.

How do I know if a situation is escalating?

So far in this book, I've shared key security terms, where threats come from, and how a targeted attack follows a process. One of the key attributes in early identification of the existence of a threat and/or person of concern. In this section, I want to share how you can identify when an issue or a problematic person escalates.

As discussed, a threat often starts with a grievance. We all have grievances, whether they are personal or professional, but rarely do we resort to violence or seek to harm the other person by destroying their reputation or causing them psychological harm.

The quicker you can identify a problematic person, the better. That may appear obvious. However, the changes in behaviour often highlight a person is escalating.

A common trend among public figures and influencers is to have their social media 'screened', eliminating at source any posts or communications that contain certain keywords or terms that are considered inappropriate. The idea is that the recipient never sees or receives the abuse or threats. There are real positives to this strategy, and it goes a long way to protect the recipient from the psychological harm that is intended. I introduced exactly that process when in Parliament and, for the record, the legislation currently in place in the UK does not require the recipient to receive the message for the offence to be completed.

However, there is a real problem with this strategy. Unless those responsible for managing the system in place review every post and are properly trained in threat assessments and can recognize the signs of escalation, there can be a real threat developing or being communicated which may go unnoticed. That can be an extremely dangerous strategy, especially when relying on AI or automation to do the job for you.

In the next chapter, I will discuss the proximal or pre-attack indicators of note. However, the Pathway to Violence (refer to Figure 6.1) discussed in the previous section is the best place to start.

Outside of the proximal and pre-attack indicators, behavioural indicators must be taken seriously.

In this section, I am going to focus on ten key behavioural indicators. These are not listed in any order, as any one of these should be considered a red flag and brought to the attention of a threat manager.

- **Multiple sources of communication:** This is when a person of concern begins communicating through one channel, such as social media, and they then move to multiple sources, such as writing letters, phone calls, and emails.
- **Suicide/homicide references:** When the communication refers to suicidal intentions, it might suggest that they no longer care about their life and are willing to sacrifice themselves. Any mention of killing someone any person should always be flagged as the fact that they are thinking of such an act is of concern.
- **Delusional/paranoid thoughts:** Any evidence from the person of concern that appears to be delusional, such as a mention of a relationship or a partnership that doesn't exist, whether personal

or business-related. This may include any suggestion that they have 'noticed' some form of messaging from your client, such as when they wear 'x', they read this as some form of communication. Any suggestions of paranoia, such as believing they are being listened to or followed, should be treated seriously.

- **Escalation of emotional state:** This may be apparent when their communications demonstrate an increase in their levels of anger or hate, perhaps in response to not being responded to or not receiving the response they wanted.

- **Erratic or drug-related behaviour:** Whether online or in person, evidence that suggests that their behaviour is constantly changing (erratic) is a concern. The presence or suspicion of drug or significant alcohol use can compound this.

- **Specific references to time, date, and location:** Because of your client's role or status, your client may publicise events you attend. However, when any reference is made to specific dates, places and times that are not in the public domain, caution must be applied. It may imply that there is an insider threat, a cyber compromise, or the event has leaked the attendance.

- **Stalking or harassment:** Any evidence of stalking or harassment includes a course of conduct, meaning there have been two or more incidents of concern. As discussed earlier in the book, there are different types of stalkers, and each must be treated seriously, at least until the typology and threat have been assessed.

- **Sudden cessation of communication:** Following on from the previous point, when a person has been communicating persistently and then suddenly stops, this may be suspicious. The more time and energy a person have committed to their unwanted pursuit, the less likely they are to stop suddenly. There may be a justifiable reason, such as illness or imprisonment. However, in the absence of this, the question must be asked: what are they now doing offline?

- **Weapons:** Any reference to possession of or interest in weapons should be treated seriously, especially where an indication of training is involved.
- **Threats of violence:** You will recall that earlier in the book, I discussed 'Hunters and Howlers' and the concept that those who make threats rarely pose threats. This is not absolute, and depending on which research you refer to, anywhere between 5% and 20% of people who make threats can pose a threat. Equally, where there has been an intimate relationship, all threats must be taken seriously.

Summary

Threat management is not about trawling the internet or communication and looking for threats. It is the process of identifying, assessing and then managing any threats. The process involves identifying a person of concern and assessing his or her behaviour. This process should not be a one-time act; it should be a constant process of evaluation. Individuals who target another rarely just snap and attack. They move from their grievance to ideation because they feel they cannot resolve it. They often follow a process referred to as The Pathway (Figure 6.1), which takes them on a journey toward their final act. This journey is not a fait accompli, as they can change their minds or be thwarted. One factor is that they may leave clues while they escalate towards the final act. These clues can be identified in their behaviours, with communication being one such behaviour. An understanding of the indicators that suggest a person is escalating should be shared with the recipient and their staff so that they recognize them and can inform their protectors. The earlier the indicators are identified the more time you will have to resolve the grievance, provide any additional security and thwart any planned attack.

Chapter 7

Pre-attack warning behaviours

Introduction

In this chapter, I am going to introduce you to the key pre-attack or proximal *warning behaviours* of an escalating threat or attack. These behaviours are seen in everyone, from stalkers to mass shooters, and some are more prevalent than others. The truth is that no matter how good someone is at conducting research on a person of concern, if they do not know, understand, and can identify these warning behaviours, they may not identify an immediate or escalating threat. These indicators are used by everyone from the US Secret Service and the FBI to the very best in behavioural threat management. They are called pre-attack or proximal (close) warning indicators. Proximal in this context refers to time rather than distance, so it refers to how close they are to an attack. These clusters of behaviours have been subject to significant academic and operational research globally over the past 40 years and are proven to work. Once you understand them, you will notice them in news stories of attacks and, much like a jigsaw, be able to piece together the journey a person goes on prior to an attack. They are not to be used to attempt to randomly predict who is going to attack but to be considered from a preventable perspective, helping to identify if a person of concern that has been brought to your attention is escalating towards a violent outcome.

The predominant thinking has identified eight pre-attack warning behaviours.[72] They are:

- pathological fixation
- the pathway to intended or targeted violence
- directly communicated threats
- last resort behaviour
- leakage
- identification
- novel aggression
- energy burst

The first three of these behaviours have already been covered in this book. In this chapter, I will introduce you to the remainder.

Last resort behaviours

We know from the last chapter that people of concern travel on a journey starting with a grievance and ending with their attack. While travelling along that pathway, they may leave clues, and one of the most significant clues is their communication of last resort. Statistically, this behaviour is seen in 64% of cases of successful attacks. As mentioned, the grievance is the starting point, and when it cannot be successfully resolved by the person of concern they make the decision that the only way they can resolve it is through an act of violence. This is where they generate their intention of violence.

This may be the first point in which they communicate their last resort behaviour. It is important to remember that communication is a behaviour. However, not all 'last resort behaviour' is evidenced through communication. It can be explicit, or quite nuanced. When a person is in communication about their grievance, they may tell you exactly when they move to the violent ideation with phrases such as.

- 'I have had enough.'
- 'You give me no other option.'

- 'You wait... I'll show you.'
- 'I'm at the end of my tether.'
- 'I have no other choice.'

In this space, they feel they are trapped and have no other option. It is considered that this is a sign of desperation and distress through 'word or deed' with the person using this to justify their actions.[73] In effect, what they are saying is: 'I must act, and I must act now.' It is time imperative as it may be that their actions are part of a broader plan to end their life. A good indicator of this is when their communications refer to any suicidal or homicidal ideation. Those are key red flags.

There are numerous examples of this 'last resort language' being used.

Case Study

On 17 June 2015, Dylan Roof, a white supremacist, attacked the Emanuel Methodist Church in Charleston, South Carolina. Before doing so, he published his 'manifesto' on his personal website titled 'lastrhodesian'. His manifesto contained this paragraph, which evidences the 'last resort' language and his feeble attempt at justifying his murderous action.[74]

'I have no choice. I am not in the position to, alone, go into the ghetto and fight. I chose Charleston because it is most historic city in my state, and at one time had the highest ratio of blacks to whites in the country.'

He then continued to justify his plot with 'We have no skinheads, no real KKK, no one doing anything but talking on the internet. Well, someone has to have the bravery to take it to the real world, and I guess that has to be me.'[75] Roof was the first person in the USA to be sentenced to death for a federal hate crime.

Case Study

Just days after Donald Trump lost the US 2020 election, white supremacist and Oath Keepers founder Stewart Rhodes sent the following message to his followers: 'Trump has one last chance, right now, to stand. But he will need us and our rifles.' This post preceded the Washington insurrection where the Capitol building was attacked on 6 January 2021.[76] While this was posted sometime before the event in mind, it infers that this is an 'end of tether' event, which in their minds it was as they believed that the end of Trump was, in fact, the end of them. The post was effectively a call to action.

Not every example of 'last resort' needs to result in such violence, nor does it have to be from a white supremacist. It can be evidence just as well in a person's behaviour rather than their communications.

Triggering events

Research tells us that events often trigger a response. The event might be political, such as an election or, as in the case study above, a politician not being elected. This can be exaggerated by political parties who predict cataclysmic events should they not be elected. Whenever you are researching a person of concern, dates must be considered. It may be that a 'watershed' event triggers the person to start planning their own events, such as the anniversary of 9/11 or a high-profile attack such as the Columbine school or the 7/7 attacks in London. (You can find details of the original attacks by searching online.) However, while they may trigger their plans to commence, they are unlikely to be the date of their planned attack. Equally, the triggering event may be personal, such as an anniversary of a significant event, such as the death of their mother or a child, or a divorce, because of its personal relevance to them. It may well be that that personal anniversary date is their attack date. The end of their life may coincide with a key personal date. (Take a look at endnote 23.)

Another triggering event might be the serving, an injunction, or another similar type of intervention, such as a letter being served on them. You might consider that this intervention will lower the risk, which it may do in time. However, the initial response to such an intervention is likely to be an escalation. For some, this intervention triggers a feeling of 'the end' or a loss of control and spurs them into action. The key here is that whenever an intervention is planned, assume the risk is going to go up and take precautionary steps; ensure all parties are aware of exactly when the person of concern is made aware and their response.

Leakage

In the previous chapter, I introduced you to the concept of the 'Hunter and Howler'. In this concept, I detailed how very few people who communicate a direct threat carry it out. In this section, I will now introduce you to what they will do: they often leak their intentions to a third party, online or to a relative. It is called *leakage*.

Leakage is one of the most common indicators and has featured in between 60% and 90% of researched attacks, but it may deliver a few false positives on its own.

What is apparent is how many attackers have leaked their intentions, and a third party has been aware of that information and yet either failed to join the dots, not taken it seriously or not known whom to report their concerns to.

Leakage is defined as 'the communication to a 3rd party of an intent to do harm to a target through an attack'.[77] Leakage doesn't have to be a clear sharing of information; it can be seen as bragging or a warning and can even be in the form of an illustration or tattoo. The concept was initially identified in the 1980s by the FBI's Behavioural Science Unit when investigating serial killers. They found that these killers were unable to suppress their beliefs, fantasies and urges, and they would at some point be shared, albeit not always obviously.[78]

Case Study

In June 2017 I was sitting in my office in Parliament when I was handed a scrap of paper by one of the team. I was told that this was a piece of information containing the details of a threat that had been shared at a closed meeting. It was a threat to kidnap and kill a Member of Parliament and a police officer. The information had been passed by an informant to a charity, and from them to another MP who had previously been involved with that charity.

The note said: 'An informant was in a pub at a National Action meeting when a friend was talking about kidnapping and killing Rosie Cooper the MP. He talked about kidnapping a police officer and killing her, too. He said he was then going to martyr himself.'

This was a clear case of leakage. The person leaking the threat was Jack Renshaw. He was a neo-Nazi white supremacist and was also being investigated for child sexual abuse offences.

Several indicators in this message suggested that this was a genuine threat rather than just someone showing off or bragging.

I contacted the head of the Domestic Counter Terrorism Unit and shared my concerns, which led to an investigation being instigated.

Jack Renshaw was later convicted of several crimes, including plotting to kill Rosie Cooper, MP, and a police officer. He received a life sentence.[79]

Case Study

A less obvious case also occurred while I was employed at Parliament. In March of 2017, an Islamic-inspired terrorist drove across Westminster Bridge, running over and killing a number of members of the public. He then abandoned his car and calmly walked into the entrance of Parliament, initially hiding in plain sight by walking with a crowd of children. He killed PC Keith Palmer before he was shot and killed.[80]

Five days before this fatal attack, Khalid Masood drove to Wales, UK, to visit his mother. In essence, this was his final goodbye and can be seen through the prism of Last Resort behaviour discussed in the previous topic. What is relevant is that as he left his mother's house, he turned to her and said, 'They'll say I'm a terrorist; I'm not.' This 'leakage' was not picked up by his mother.

Case Study

Teenager Liam Lyburd was arrested in November 2014 after a woman he had been chatting to on Facebook became increasingly worried about what he had been posting. When the police raided his home, they found an arsenal of weapons, including a handgun and ammunition. He had been planning to attack his former school, which had expelled him in 2012.[81] He had posted images of himself wearing a balaclava and holding a gun.

In a chat with a girl in a shop, he stated: 'You will see me on the news covered in blood with my brain on the other side of the room.' Another read: 'I'm going to die along with my friends in school. It's so sad, my life. I'm going to kill my mum and the kids in my school – it's going to be amazing.'

Thankfully, in this case others engaging with Lyburd online were sufficiently alarmed to contact the police.[82] During the investigation, a deleted file was recovered from his computer. The note contained further evidence of his thoughts and how he intended to take revenge against the school that had expelled him. It said: 'You people ruined my whole life, don't expect me to show mercy today. No one disrespects me and gets away with it. I'll teach you people a little lesson on respect with my 9mm jacketed hollow points. It's time for extreme civil disobedience.

'Fantasy will become reality today for sure. Where the mind goes, the body will follow, and, yes, people will die; there's no question about that.'

Police also found webcam pictures he took of himself dressed for combat, armed with a Glock and brandishing a knife. As police took away Lyburd, he laughed and told officers they had saved lives, preventing what would have been a massacre at the college.

He was later convicted of a number of serious offences and, in 2015, sentenced to life imprisonment.

Motivation

People leak their thoughts and plans for different reasons.

Research suggests that there is rarely a single motive for their leakage. They leak because they are excited, they want to frighten or intimidate, seeking attention, to elicit a sense of power, and for some they just can't hold back telling someone. What this research does suggest, however, is that the leakage should not be seen as some form of remorse or motivated by a desire to be caught or stopped (you can refer back to endnote 73 for more information). In recent times, it has become the norm to release some form of 'manifesto' for others to read their justification and perhaps with the intent to motivate others.

One piece of very visual evidence from the 7/7 terrorist bombings in London in 2005 was the videos released by the terrorists. Filmed before the attack and using past tense language, they sought to justify their actions. This form of leakage also ensures that they are identified and remembered. They want their deaths to mean something. Their videos also provided proof of the presence of other indicators such as fixation, identification and the pathway to violence.

Early identification and recognition of leakage in any threat assessment is crucial. By recognizing signs of leakage, you may then go on to identify other indicators present, as I did in the Rosie Cooper threat, which provides further evidence of a planned attack. Without looking for additional leakage or other warning behaviours, the evaluation of leakage may be a false positive and provide an inaccurate assessment. (Again, endnote 73 will be useful here.)

Identification

The next topic is titled *Identification*. This is another key indicator, and when I reviewed attacks on UK politicians, this one was the most prevalent. It has two separate parts to it.

The first is where individuals want to feel part of something bigger than themselves; they believe they are 'soldiers for a cause'. This is referred to as the *warrior mentality* or *pseudo commando*.

The second part is where they sometimes study and copy previous attackers often seeking to emulate them.

Signs of identification can be seen in everyday life, from tattoos of a football team, a military unit, or a gang to flags flown outside a house or on a protest march.

One of the key elements that can signify escalation within identification is a person's movement from a belief to an identity. Where once they believe in something, a movement, or an ideology, they now move from believing in it to becoming a part of it, and this then forms an identity. They move from *I believe* to *I am*. It evidences that they have moved from what they think about all day (fixation) to who they have become (self-identity). This movement is a key prediction of violence. This move can be seen in their fixation and interest in other attacks and attackers, weapons, tactics, law enforcement and other paraphernalia.[83]

Case Study

In 1999, David Copeland,[84] a British bomber, targeted three minority communities over three successive weekends. He evidenced this move from belief to identity very well when he stated:

'Why, why, why can't someone blow that place up? That'd be a good one, you know, that would piss everyone off… (this thought) kept going around, floating around my head, day after day after day.

'And then after a while I became that thought, you know, I was going to do it.'

What he appears to be saying is that initially he was thinking about the attacks as a concept, but he moved from it being a belief to it being his identity. He had become a pseudo warrior.

Case Study

During the 1980s, there were three significant attacks on public figures, which demonstrates the concept of identification. In 1980, Mark Chapman shot and killed John Lennon outside of

Lennon's home in New York. Chapman had been stalking Lennon for some time. He had read the book *The Catcher in the Rye*. So enamoured was he with the main character Holden Caulfield that he unsuccessfully tried to change his name by deed poll. When he had shot Lennon, Chapman sat down on the curb, pulled out his copy of the book and began to read it until the police arrested him.

Four months later, John Hinckley Jr attempted to assassinate President Ronald Reagan when he was leaving a hotel. Interestingly, Hinckley's motivation was that he was in love with, and had been stalking, Jodie Foster for some years.

Prior to leaving his hotel room to kill Reagan, Chapman wrote to Foster (leakage), telling her what he was about to do was the greatest demonstration of love ever. When Hinckley was apprehended, he also was in possession of the book *The Catcher in the Rye*.

Nine years later, Robert Bardo killed the young television actress Rebecca Schaeffer at her apartment in Hollywood. He had been stalking her for three years. He also had a copy of *The Catcher in the Rye* when he murdered Schaeffer, which he tossed onto the roof of a building as he fled. While he was adamant that he had not been emulating Chapman, this was later contradicted by Chapman, who stated he had been corresponding with Bardo prior to the shooting.[85]

The presence of the book *The Catcher in the Rye* is not a coincidence; it is evidence of emulation or copycatting. It is as if there was something about the book that the latter two attackers were connecting to Chapman's attack on Lennon.

When researching a person of concern, be aware of such connections to previous attackers. Alternatively, if there is something that stands out as being odd, investigate further to see whether it is connected to other attackers.

Case Study

A good example of a person becoming a pseudo-commando is Anders Behring Breivik. On 22 July 2011, Breivik committed mass murder in Norway.[86] He is arguably the textbook case of many of the indicators referenced in this book. Despite having never served in the military, law enforcement or any other uniformed organization, Breivik dressed up in a wetsuit with military insignia while armed with a rifle with various sights, a dress uniform with medals and insignia, a masonic outfit, and a HAZMAT suit with insignia of the Knights Templar. He created all the outfits he wore, adorned with various insignia of Nazism and other features. He also identified with the Knights Templers, an eleventh-century force that combatted the rise of Islam, that he signed off his manifesto the night before he carried out his attack with 'Sincere regards, Anders Breivik, Justiciar Knight Commander, Templar Europe, Knights Templar Norway'.

Visual indicators such as the wearing of uniforms, gang tattoos, flags, and others such items are all potential indicators of identification. The key is very often the context in which these appear.

As well as emulating the US domestic terrorist Timothy McVeigh, Breivik spent 17 hours a day for two years playing on a computer war game in which he became the leader, giving him an elevated pseudo-commando status. (The case study in endnote 87 gives details.)

The fact that these individuals copy other attackers shouldn't be too much of a surprise. It is the feeling they have of being connected with them and seeking to be better than those they emulate.

Almost every time we have a 'lone wolf' attack, we are left with some form of a manifesto, written or video, in which the individual associates themselves with a wider ideology, be that ISIS/ISIS/Daesh or a right-wing group. Invariably, the 'group' claims the individual despite having never heard of them, as it seeks to promote their movement. The individual's association is to signify that their actions had meaning, and they were a 'soldier' of that cause. The last thing they want to be seen to be is meaningless, as that may be the very emotion that drove them to carry out the act.

The nature of the identification may help you understand where their threat lies. A person of concern who has tattoos or refers to the extreme right-wing, Nazism or the like is probably going to target and attack minority communities. Conversely, an individual emulating or identifying with the extreme elements of Islamist beliefs is likely to attack a different target. This can be evidenced in the behaviour of Nidal Hasan, who conducted the 2009 Fort Hood US military base attack.

Case Study

Major Nidal Hasan was a US Army Medical Corps psychiatrist. Originally from Palestine but growing up in the USA, his family were considered more 'culturally' Muslim than devout followers.

In 2001, he moved home to look after his mother who was dying from cancer. It was at this time that he began to worry about the state of her soul in the afterlife. His family owned a shop that sold alcohol, and Hasan began to believe that alcohol was a mortal sin. He believed that, because of this, his mother would burn eternally in hell. He considered the only way to prevent this was for him to change his own life and beliefs to be a more devout Muslim. Over the next few years, he became increasingly extreme in his beliefs, which included him engaging online with extremist preachers. In the years preceding the attack on Fort Hood, his behaviour changed so dramatically that he fell out with family members whom he criticized for their dress and behaviour. In essence, his entire identity changed. This was visible in how he dressed, behaved, talked and even in the lectures he gave at work. This culminated in, rather than pledging his allegiance to the US flag while dressed in his uniform, he pledged his allegiance to the Koran. He no longer identified as a US soldier; he now identified as a soldier of Allah. The volume of evidence that should have raised red flags was ignored. The trigger for his attack was his posting to Afghanistan. His terrorist attack at Fort Hood on 5 November 2009, left 13 killed, 32 injured and countless other lives forever changed.[87]

Lesser indictors

The final two indicators are *Novel Aggression* and *Energy Burst*.

Novel Aggression is defined as an aggressive act that the person of concern carries out to test their ability to carry out their ultimate desired aim. They want to be sure that when faced with the opportunity they seek, they can act in the way they want to do. Very often, this act can be totally unrelated to the final act they are planning, as the act itself is not connected to the motivation or grievance they have. This act of novel aggression can often be missed by those researching the person of concern due to a lack of connection with the investigation. The act itself can also have been carried out some time ago, so it doesn't have to be a recent event. Its purpose is to ensure the person can commit a random act of violence. The act may vary from killing an animal, carrying out an act of criminal damage or a random attack on a person. It may also involve testing their ability to cope under arrest. While it was historically usual for a person to have to leave their home to carry out an act of novel aggression, more recently, it is believed that online first-person war games may provide the necessary validation. Breivik was known to have played such games almost obsessionally for two years. This behaviour will also tie in those who are loners and who through the possibility of being on the autistic spectrum lack the social skills required and therefore spend a significant amount of time indoors gaming. The act of gaming, to the degree that some of these individuals do, may act to desensitize them so that they are more capable of acting violently without any moral compass detracting them from acting.

Case Study

On 22 October 2014, Michael Zehaf-Bibeau killed Corporal Nathan Cirillo and injured three others before he attacked the Canadian Parliament. His acts of Novel Aggression are believed to have happened as long before as three years. In December 2011, he walked into the Royal Canadian Mounted Police (RCMP) field office in Burnaby, British Columbia and confessed to an armed robbery he had committed a decade earlier. No such robbery is reported to have occurred. Interestingly, the very next night, he attempted a robbery at a McDonald's restaurant armed only with a pencil. He then waited for the police to arrive. Were these acts to test and see how the police responded and whether he could test himself?

The final behaviour of concern is called *Energy Burst*. Described as the most difficult behaviour to identify, it is essentially a flurry of activity carried out before an attack. It is suggested that to identify this behaviour accurately, you must first know the person's baseline or ordinary behaviour. What you may consider to be a 'flurry' may be normal to the person of concern. The key is that this behaviour must be close to the final act; it is them getting prepared and putting their house in order.

Case Study

Jared Lee Loughner is an American mass murderer who pleaded guilty to 19 charges of murder and attempted murder in connection with the 8 January 2011 Tucson killing spree.[88,89]

His activity in the hours before the attack may have alerted others to the impending attack as he went into an 'Energy Burst'.

The timeline of his activities is as follows:

- Just before midnight on 7 January, he drops off 35mm film at Walgreen.
- Shortly after midnight, he checked into a Motel 6. He then began searching the web for 'assassins' and 'lethal injection'.
- 0219hrs: picks up the photos and makes a purchase. Leaves a phone message with a friend.
- 0412hrs: posts to Myspace photo of Glock and the words 'Goodbye Friends' (leakage).
- 0600hrs: visits Walmart and Circle K stores.
- 0727hrs Unable to purchase ammunition at 1st Walmart purchases 9mm full metal jacket ammo and a diaper bag.
- 0730hrs: stopped by police for running a red light before returning home, where he argued with his father before running away.
- 0941hrs: returns to Circle K; gets a cab. He then goes to a supermarket where he insists on getting the correct change for a cab ride.
- 16 mins later, at 10:10 hrs, he opened fire, killing six and wounding a further 13, including US Representative Gabby Giffords (shot her in the head).

He was wrestled to the ground by bystanders. A sheriff's deputy who detained him five minutes later found 30 rounds of ammunition, a knife and a plastic bag containing money in his pockets.

While Novel Aggression and Energy Burst are the least likely of the pre-attack behaviours to be identified, they are still noticeable in some. The challenge with identifying these behaviours will be joining the dots. That said, should you identify an unusual violent act that seems out of character and/or a flurry of activity with regards to a person of concern, I'd suggest that rather than dismissing these as nothing to concern yourself with, take a deeper look!

Summary

The term *warning behaviors* was used to suggest that the person of concern had changed their behaviour and was on a period of acceleration towards the attack. They do not predict who will attack, but they suggest an increasing threat. They can be useful to help threat assessors manage low-frequency intentional acts of violence towards an identified target. The theory argues that there are eight warning behaviours. It doesn't suggest that they all will or need to be present, but clearly the greater the cluster, the greater the threat. For the benefit of clarity, should any of the warning behaviours be identified, the person of concern should be brought to the attention of law enforcement or your security lead.

The final act does not have to be an act of violence. It may be an act to cause reputational harm, a non-violent workplace incident or other insider threat activities.

Chapter 8

Safer events and functions

Introduction

Increasingly, events and function are critical areas of risk. Whether these are small private functions or huge events hosting global icons and sports teams or a business conference, there are commonalities that must be considered and managed. Events and functions are a target for terrorists, fixated people, criminals, business adversaries and, for different reasons, the media. A poorly managed event or function risks significant physical, financial, psychological and reputational harm. Event security requires detailed planning and an understanding of the various areas of vulnerability together with the methodology of mitigating each area. In my former career as a Metropolitan Police officer, I was part of a small cadre of Counter Terrorist Security Coordinators, known as a CT SecCo. According to the College of Policing, a CT SecCo is responsible for the development of a security plan with a view to minimizing, managing and mitigating risk in respect of an event or operation involving members of the Royal Family, Government or other specified high-profile events.[90]

One event where security was compromised was the Ariana Grande concert in Manchester, England, on 22 May 2017, resulting in the deaths of 22 people with a further 1,017 people being injured. One of the victims of the terrorist bombing was Martyn Hett. Martyn's mother, Figen Murray, subsequently led a campaign to improve security at public venues and events, resulting in an impending new piece of legislation known as Martyn's Law. This law, when finally passed, will require venues and event organizers to put in place measures to protect the public from terrorist attacks. This new law is necessary, as despite several companies promoting and practising event and public area security, few have been properly trained in identifying and countering risks involved. This chapter will provide some insight into this subject and will assist any security professionals who are tasked with protecting an event, a function or a public area.

The first step in conducting an event security plan is to have a threat assessment completed. Without a threat assessment, you will not know how high the threat is, and which of the attack methodologies might be likely. When securing a private function for a high profile or high net worth person, the threat will be very different to that posed to a government minister or member of a Royal Family. For an event including members of the Royal Family or senior government officials, the parameters should include plan to consider the threat from a sniper as far as you can see. For a private function, a counter-sniper plan is probably not be necessary at all.

When conducting an event security plan where the focus may be a music or sporting act, be mindful of which other high profile or prominent people are attending. The target may not be the main act, it might be others, or it may be to cause terror and panic by attacking the attendees or the local community. It is critical that your plan looks to maintain the safety of all, including those on the fringes.

The plan must include three phases: the period leading up to the event including when the attendees and the act arrive; the event itself; and the period when all those present leave, which will include the disruption to the local community.

The threat assessment must also be mindful of any unwanted attention from fixated people, stalkers and 'superfans' who desire proximity and may have turned up at previous venues. This will be a critical factor when briefing and debriefing the staff employed at the events.

Once you have satisfied the level of threat posed to your event or the key principles, you can then decide the level of security required. If you do not understand the level of threat, you may find it a challenge to persuade the organizers what resources are required. Should you to decide to assume that the threat is high, you may struggle to increase the resources should a new threat be communicated.

The threat level helps dictate what is necessary and proportionate to mitigate each threat. Events and functions organizers will seek to reduce the level of security required, partly due to cost and partly due the atmosphere of the event. An event with a heavy security presence may cause the attendees to be anxious, reducing their enjoyment and perhaps persuading some not to turn up.

The Royal Family will never cancel an event due to security, so the police can continuingly add extra police officers and resources. That isn't the same in a commercial setting, where the police may recommend that the event should be cancelled for safety's sake together with the excessive costs being prohibitive.

When an event takes place, several differing security roles are engaged. They may include:

- a close protection team looking after the principal person or celebrity act
- venue search teams
- guest or attendee bag search
- in-house stewards and security
- cyber security team
- counter-reconnaissance team
- crowd control
- parking control and vehicle removal

- counter-sniper teams
- external stewards
- crime prevention and detection.

The critical role is the security professional who acts as the single point of contact (SPOC), and who coordinates the security planning.

At a large event, you may decide to allocate each threat area, or attack methodology to a different member of your team, but you remain the SPOC.

There are several attack methodologies that must be considered and where vulnerabilities exist, mitigated. These include:

- vehicle-based attack
- insider threat
- human threat, such as lone actor
- targeted attack from a fixated person
- improvized explosive attack, including CBRN
- distance attack, such as sniper
- activists or protestors
- technical attack, such as cyber
- airborne attack, such as from a UAV/drone
- criminal acts.

The targets of an attack must all be considered and accounted for. These will include the act or significant persons, the attendees, the staff employed, media, and those in the immediate vicinity such as passers-by and neighbours.

Invacuating or evacuation?

Most people are familiar with an evacuation plan, in which we are required to leave the location we are in and head to a designated point.

An evacuation point, if known, can be targeted as a secondary target and so cannot be assumed to be safe.

There are occasions when the threat is external to the place you are protecting and, in those circumstances, rather than evacuate people towards the threat, you will do the opposite and bring them into what should be a safer place.

Critical to the success of this is the communication plan. How, in the moment of the chaos will you ensure that people know to either remain where they are or evacuate to a safe place. This communication strategy must be thought through and planned.

Vehicle-based attack

A vehicle can be used to conduct an attack or to deliver a device, such as an explosive device, to the venue.

Car-ramming attacks, or vehicular assaults, in which drivers deliberately drive their vehicles into public gatherings, pedestrians or bicyclists, have become an increasingly common terrorist tactic. Historically, both Al-Qaeda and ISIS have urged the use of vehicles to mow down pedestrians. As well as the physical impact of mass casualties, the act creates fear and panic, causing crowds to disperse in multiple uncontrolled directions in which the terrorist can hide.

A vehicle can be used to carry or position an explosive device close to the target or can be used to deliver a suicide attacks.

Wherever possible the vicinity of the event should be a vehicle free zone. For large-scale public events this may include the use of road closures, with any vehicles parked in the designated free zone being removed. This may also be supported by hostile vehicle mitigation (HMV) systems.[91] By delaying their actions, HVM systems offer valuable time for alarms to be raised and counter-terrorism measures to be activated.

Where HMV solutions are not available, alternative options might include using other vehicles to block routes.

An alternative may be to enable vetted and searched vehicles with facilities to park within the identified zone.

Insider threat

The threat from an insider is one that created concern for every security plan. Organizations are often concerned that an insider leaks valuable privileged information, enables a cyber attack, or facilitates hostile actors access to a secure environment.

During the foiled attack plan of the Taylor Swift concert in Austria in August 2024, it was identified that one of the terrorists involved had secured employment at the venue.[92] Whenever conducting a security review for a forthcoming event, this vulnerability must be high on the agenda. This can be managed by requesting the details of all staff employed during a planned event, requesting the details of any new staff within a specific timeframe and details of any staff who have left. This must include details of any staff who left disgruntled or with a grievance.

When agency staff are being used, details of their due diligence process is important.

All staff being employed at an event, including where internal existing staff are being used for a smaller private event, must be accounted for. It can be good practice to ensure they are issued with a wrist band at the beginning of each shift and returned when they go off duty. This prevents the wrist band being shared and unverified staff accessing the event.

Human threat, such as lone actor

An obvious threat is people. Whether they are lone actor terrorists, activists, fixated people, superfans and criminals such as drug dealers or the media, people pose a threat.

Most people are used to being searched before they board an aircraft and when entering certain premises, such as a nightclub or courtroom. The subject of searching requires more thought than it is sometimes given. When seeking to secure a venue, one of the practical systems is to incorporate a bag drop facility. By requiring attendees to deposit their bags beyond a certain size seeks to achieve several objectives. First, it prevents attendees from bring an explosive device into the venue in their bags. However, what is doesn't do is prevent an explosive device being deposited at the bag drop site, which means the bag drop site must be some distance from the venue.

A search regime can be used to search people, identifying whether attendees and staff are carrying weapons, drugs, and prohibited items such as cameras (where they are banned) listening devices, spray paint, banners, flags and other items depending on the event.

Improvized explosive attack (IED), including CBRN

An IED can be a hugely sophisticated device or something simpler made from a firework. Devices can be homemade using items such as pipes or pressure cookers and can be made more dangerous with the use of nails, bolts or scrap metal which then acts as a means of causing more injuries due to fragmentation. When toxins are included, the IED can create a chemical, biological or radiological risk, spreading contamination.

An IED can also be designed to ignite (rather than explode) to initiate a fire.

The terrorist group known as the Irish Republican Army (IRA) demonstrated in 1984 that they could plant a device three weeks in advance designed to kill the then-UK Prime Minister Margaret Thatcher and the government of the day. The device was fitted with a long-delay timer, such as the type used in video-cassette recorders. The timing unit was battery powered and a timer was also incorporated into the device.[93]

The level of sophistication will have increased over the past 40 years, which means that any security plan must be alive to the risks posed.

Equally, homemade IEDs caused significant harm and death to UK military and allies during the Afghanistan conflict, so devices do not have to be highly technical.

The presence of an IED can be countered by a professional counter-terrorism search team, with the help from explosive detection dogs and explosive trace detectors (ETDs) that can detect small amounts of explosives, vapours or residue.

Distance attack, such as sniper

Former US President, Donald Trump, was the subject of an assassination attempt at a political rally in Butler, Pennsylvania in July 2024.[94] The source of the attack was a lone sniper operating from an elevated position on a warehouse roof with an AR-15 style rifle some 140 metres (400 feet) from the podium. The weapon was legally purchased in the US.

It would be highly unlikely that a potential shooter could source such a weapon in the UK, although such a weapon might come from an illegal source. Other types of distance weapons, such as a mortar, grenades or a rocket-propelled grenade are equally unlikely to be acquired in the UK. However, it would not be the first such attack in the UK. The IRA launched three homemade mortar shells at 10 Downing Street, the residence of the UK Prime Minister, to assassinate the then-PM, who was meeting his cabinet to discuss the Gulf War.[95]

To conduct such an attack in the UK would require significant planning and skills, and the likelihood of such an attack remains low. To counter such an attack, the security plan must identify potential firing positions and deploy resources to secure that position. A further deployment of a counter-sniper team, to maintain vigilance and to provide fire at a potential attacker, is quite normal at events in which a Police CT SecCo is tasked.

Activist or protestors?

The UK has seen an increase of direct action by activists and protest groups in recent years. They have successful breached the security and gained access to the UK Parliament, Heathrow Airport, plus other venues including museums and financial establishments as well as targeted events where they believe their adversaries are attending.

In general, what they seek is publicity and they achieve that by damaging and destroying property, embarrassing public officials and blockading access.

A security plan must account for this type of attack methodology. It is critical to understand the likelihood of such action by knowing who is attending the event/function and by understanding any connection to activities that may attract protest activity.

This can be furthered by including an OSINT (Open-Source Intelligence) investigation and monitoring as part of the plan.

Physical searches of those attending events may identify those who intend to seek publicity with banners and items to commit criminal damage.

Technical attacks

A technical attack tends to include the use of IT. This will often fall under the label of a cyber attack. It is critical to recognize that these attacks can take control of elevators, traffic lights, alarm systems, as well as the disruption of utilities and communication systems.

This type of attack has wider implications. If the security regime is considered impregnable, then alternative is to cause the attendees to exit the venue. A technical attack can cause the alarm systems to activate causing an evacuation. If the attacker knows where the muster point for an evacuation is, they can target their attack at that unprotected site.

It is critical to check when Wi-Fi codes have been changed, whether there is a secondary evacuation point and whether there are back-up systems. Where such an attack is likely, including cyber security, professionals familiar with the systems on to the security team is critical.

Airborne attack, such as from a UAV/drone

During a campaign rally in Dresden in 2013, a UAV flew within feet of German Chancellor Angela Merkel. The UAV hovered in front of her briefly before crashing into the stage. Fortunately, it was harmless. It could, however, have been carrying an explosive payload, or it could be filming the private party of a high-profile celebrity.

There are several tactics that can be deployed to counter the threat from a UAD. At large-scale events, no-fly zones can be introduced. The UK has several airspace restrictions these apply equally to, both unmanned and manned aircraft. These areas are referred to as: Prohibited Areas, Restricted Areas or Danger Areas. There are also strict rules controlling who can fly a UAV and where it can be flown.

There are several commercial counter-unmanned aerial system (C-UAS) technologies used to detect, track and identify potential threat drones, and then apply a counter-measure effect. UAV technology is constantly developing, and for that reason I would encourage security professionals to engage with a specialist where concerns exist.

Criminal acts

Whenever a major event is planned, the criminal fraternity must also be accounted for. It might be your assumption that this will be a policing issue, and to some degree that is correct. However, while the police will be responsible for the external criminality, the police presence inside the venue will be limited. The types of criminality that will be a threat will include:

- ticket touts
- drugs
- theft
- counterfeit merchandise
- sexual offences.

Your security plan must include methods to combat and manage these criminal acts, and the abstraction of security staff involved in their detection and the liaison with law enforcement.

Any security plan is fluid and therefore you must build in flexibility in the event of the threat assessment increasing or changing, requiring you to identify a different use of your resources.

Case Study

In the early hours of one morning my phone rang. I was informed that intelligence has been reported indicating that a member of staff at the venue of a Royal visit had failed to turn up for work. Further enquiries identified that this person of concern had possession of the building's keys and that, having conducted an intelligence investigation, the person had a connection with a terrorist group.

The question the senior officer in charge (known as Gold) wanted to know was: What was I going to do about this intelligence? How would it affect my plan?

I had spent considerable time coordinating the security plan and had submitted a detailed report to Gold a few days previously.

My response was that I wasn't going to be changing anything at this stage. Our plan included a detailed search plan, including a full search by a police search team supported by explosive detection dogs and explosive trace detectors. I was confident that, had a device been planted, we would find it. I initiated further investigations of the missing worker, tasking officers to visit their home and talk with their family to better understand the situation. I briefed the search team of the intelligence and encouraged greater focus. I then spoke with the close protection officer of the member of the Royal Family due to be visiting the event later that day, who was satisfied with the plan.

Our investigations later identified that the missing worker had been unwell.

The event was a success, with the member of the Royal Family attending, and the hosts happy with the day.

Summary

The events industry is a growing industry. The UK events industry is a world leader in staging events across the world. As a sector, it is currently worth £39.1 billion to the UK economy. This doesn't account for the number of private functions that members of the private client and UHNW community host.

Paid-for and business events, crowded places and public fixtures, are attractive targets to terrorists, criminals, activists and fixated people. Private events are attractive to criminals and the media.

It is likely that Martyn's Law will be enacted by 2025 and new protocols will be introduced.

The training of security risk managers involved in events planning is at best mixed, and greater professionalism is welcome.

It is critical that those involved in planning the security for such events understand the attacks methodologies, and the importance of having a proper threat assessment to work to.

Without that, it becomes little more than guesswork. New and evolving threats will continue to challenge security professionals, with cyber security and the growing use of UAVs still requiring better solutions.

Despite the existence of industry security professionals and policing collaborating to protect events, attacks still occur, with the attempted assassination of former US President Donald Trump a recent example. If the US Secret Service can fail, then so can we all.

It is for that reason I recommend the adoption of the CT SecCo protocol of having a SPOC to coordinate all the various security issues into one place, overseen by one person with overall responsibility.

PART 2

Managing the threats

The next section of this book moves away from the threats and towards the solutions. When I first started Defuse, one of my key influences was that many 'clients' I had engaged with when in the police were provided with lots of protective security, and yet still didn't feel safe. This was a failure in security for me. The whole point of security is to feel safer, and while it is relatively simple to be safe, feeling safer can be more complicated.

One of the challenges of feeling unsafe is that the psychological impact of that can cause paranoia and hypervigilance, which will result in perceiving threats where they may not be real.

You might assume that someone highly trained in martial arts feels safer, and for some, that may be true. Many, however, will recognize that their skillset may be very productive in a dojo, less so on the street at night. Equally, in the real world, there are few rules when it comes to feeling safe, and thankfully, few have ever actually been in a violent confrontation.

We are now in the digital age, and many worry about how much of their private information is publicly accessible and how many adversaries are researching them. The truth for most, if not all of us is that there is a great deal more private information out there than most of us realize or feel comfortable with, and yet we seldom do anything about that.

Feeling safe is no longer focused on physical safety; our reputations are now under attack. Many public figures worry more about their reputation and privacy than anything else, and we have probably all heard of at least one 'celebrity' that has been 'cancelled' overnight for something published, whether factually true or not.

By the end of this section and by the end of the book, I hope that you are aware of the risks and threats out there and wiser about how you can feel safer despite them.

Chapter 9

Interviewing and gathering information

Introduction

Interviewing is a critical skill for security professionals. In my career I have interviewed murderers, terrorists, organized criminals, rapists and child abusers, informants and agents disclosing secrets, as well as more routine offenders. I have also interviewed victims of horrendous offences and eyewitnesses to deeply traumatic events. Some of them have been willing participants, while others have been anything but! I have been trained in advanced interview techniques, and specialist child abuse interviews. There are some common denominators consistent throughout all these interviews. In this chapter, I'll share what the difference between an interview and an interrogation is, what the purpose of an interview is, together with some of the critical factors in a successful interview.

Interviewing and information gathering are critical skills for all security professionals, no matter what role. Whether operating as a door supervisor, a residential security or close protection officer, or as an investigator, asking questions and establishing facts are skills that are important – and ones we can all improve on.

An interview is a structured conversation where one participant asks questions, and the other provides answers. There are numerous types of interviews, from a job interview to a suspect interview, numerous types of witness and victim interviews and intelligence interviews.

When done properly, the purpose of an interview is fact finding, information gathering or to establish the truth.

Interviewing can be a critical element to personal safety as it enables the skilled interviewer to ensure they properly understand the issues, they have accurately gathered the required information be it evidential or intelligence, and because listening is a critical element, it ensures you are better equipped to identify the indicators referred to in Part 1 of this book.

Bias

The greatest obstacle in conducting a professional interview is bias. When you go into an interview with bias the process is flawed. There are several types of bias, including confirmation bias, unconscious bias, personal biases (often referred to as prejudices) and verification bias to name just a few. When conducting an interview, confirmation bias is a critical factor.

It might be argued that we all experience bias. When interviewing a suspect, that person has already been detained for the purpose of that interview, and therefore there exists bias.

During the latter part of my police career an instruction was circulated that investigators should assume that all victims were telling the truth. This was, in my view, an extremely dangerous position to take and one that is contrary to a professional investigation.

Operation Midland was a flawed investigation that focused on allegations of child sexual abuse by Carl Beech against several high-profile British citizens – politicians, military officers and heads of security.[96] One of the critical flaws detectives made was to fully accept the allegations made by Carl Beech without objectively investigating the credibility of his claims. Their confirmation bias assumed he was telling the truth, when in fact he wasn't. Beech was subsequently convicted of 12 counts of perverting the course of justice and one count of fraud, alongside the child sex offences he had committed, and sentenced to 18 years in prison.

Interviews and indeed all investigations should be conducted with an open, inquisitive mind. Deviating from that perspective reduces the chances of identifying the truth. The purpose of an interview is not to acquire a confession.

Interviews are conducted between two people, and it is important to recognize that there in an inequality where the person conducting the interview is often the dominant person. They decide where and when the interview takes place, what time breaks occur and when the interview ends. Interviews are invariably stressful, and while much of that stress is focused on the person being interviewed, the interviewers will also experience stress. They may be under pressure to solve a case, to establish the truth, to recruit a candidate, find a missing person or identify a threat.

Acknowledging any bias that you may have is the first step, which together with a properly planned interview strategy will help to counter any biases.

Rapport

It is a well-established fact that effective interviews require rapport to be built, and this poses a problem. Too often, interviewers will enter a clumsy dance of rapport building, appearing to be interested in the person being interviewed when they are obviously not. In criminal interviews, the legal representative will attempt to interrupt any rapport-building to prevent the client from unwillingly revealing information.

Bram B. van der Meer holds a post-doctoral education program in investigative psychology. During our conversation on my Defuse Podcast (in an episode titled The Science Behind Interviewing), Bram stated it's very important for every interviewer to put himself or herself in the shoes of the person being interviewed. He went on to say that a good interviewer is not somebody who necessarily formulates great questions but somebody who can show empathy and understanding.

The first step in a good interview is to help the person being interviewed to feel comfortable. A good interview should feel like a conversation, rather than a battery of questions. The research that Bram and others have completed suggests that good interviews are planned and have a strategy.

The strategy should break the interview down into topics. The topics must be relevant and should start with the rapport building. This is only effective if you are genuinely interested in the other person. The interview should then move through the topics identified in what should feel like a conversational manner. This will only be achieved if you are inquisitive and open minded. A critical skill of any interviewer is to be a good listener. If you are so focused on your next question that you fail to listen to what the interviewee is saying, you may miss vital information and you will telegraph your lack of interest.

Types of questions

There are two key types of question used in an interview: *open* and *closed*. Both types are useful and can be used collaboratively.

A closed question is one that elicits a *yes, no* or *don't know* response. An open question requires a more detailed response. A good use of a closed question is to confirm a detail; it can also be used to ascertain truthfulness when you know the answer to the question.

As an example, you may ask a closed question such as: 'Do you work here?'

If the answer is 'Yes', you might follow up with an open question such as: 'Which department do you work in?'

This question isn't one that can be answered *yes* or *no*, and therefore requires the interviewee to provide more detail.

A properly planned interview can help you to identify when to ask closed or open questions.

Body language

As humans we unconsciously read each other's body language and, from that, we interpret emotions, positions of hierarchy and the threat they pose. Contrary to what some may believe, there is no magic formula for establishing whether someone is telling the truth or not. What we can tell, however, is whether they are comfortable or uncomfortable. While we all behave differently and will have our own idiosyncrasies that betray, disclose, divulge and reveal what we are thinking unconsciously or otherwise, there are well-researched common 'tells' that identify changes from the status quo. The subject of body language is beyond the parameters of this book, but one that I think is well worth any security professional investing time in learning. I'd recommend reading work by zoologist and ethologist Desmond Morris and by former FBI agent Joe Navarro.

As important as it is to understand the body language of those you are interviewing, it is also important to recognize what body language you may be leaking, as this may influence the response of the interview. When eliciting information, your body language may encourage the person you're interviewing to provide information that may not be accurate, but apparently pleases you.

A multi-sensory approach

When interviewing witnesses or a victim there is a tendency to ask them what they saw. This is problematic for several reasons.

First, while we all experience life through our senses, we prioritize them differently. Some people will see the world primarily through their visual senses (seeing), others through their auditory senses (hearing), while others will be more their physical senses (touch, feel, smell and taste).

Second, many people confronted by a traumatic experience will close their eyes. In essence they are shutting out the experience.

When interviewing, it is critical to use multi-sensory questions, such as:

> What did you see?
>
> What did you hear?
>
> What did you smell?

There is some evidence that the way we speak can infer our sensory preferences, with visual people speaking quickly as if their mouth is trying to keep up with the visual images they create. Kinaesthetic people are often quieter and speak slowly, suggesting they are more in 'touch' with the impact their words have, so they speak slowly to think about what they are saying. Auditory often have melodic, rhythmic voices, as their hearing is their primary sense.

Case Study

I was interviewing a victim of a violent rape. During the attack she had closed her eyes to shut out the experience, so was unable to provide any detail of what her attacker looked like. By asking multi-sensory questions, the victim was able to identify that the suspect wearing a particular cologne she recognized. She identified that he smelled of Kouros cologne. She was also able to recall that the attacker had a scab on his left forearm.

When we arrested a suspect, it was apparent that he had an injury to his left forearm, and when we searched his home, he had the cologne Kouros in his bathroom. There was further evidence that helped secure a conviction, and a long custodial sentence. Despite not 'seeing' her attacker, her other senses were absorbing other information.

Summary

Interviewing is a skill, and while some of us are better at it than others, we can all improve.

The first phase of any interview is the planning phase. It is critical to understand what the purpose of the interview is. You then plan the interview, establish what is already known and what information is sought. It is during this phase that you acknowledge any biases, such as thinking the person is responsible or an accomplice.

Planning the interview also involves identifying where it will take place and preparing that location, ensuring any refreshments are on hand and that you have any items of evidence you need.

The next phase is the rapport-building phase. This key stage ensures you reduce any stress or concerns that exist and demonstrate empathy and real interest in the person being interviewed. You are now ready to start the questioning phase, with your structured open and closed questions.

Once you have completed your questions you conclude by confirming a detail elicited.

Chapter 10

Be situationally aware

Introduction

Being situational aware is the number one skill that will keep you and your clients safe. It is a skill that many learn if they grow up in an environment that involves risks. If you grow up in a city where crime is high, drugs are rife and violence is the currency, you will unconsciously learn how to behave, recognize the signs to look out for, body language changes that suggest threats, and your intuition for risk and threats will be high. Conversely, if you grew up in a safe rural environment, many of those signs will be alien to you. This is the same when travelling, visiting other countries and experiencing different cultures; it may take time to recognize the new signs, pick up the ambience and feel safe.

Situational awareness is a skill that can be learned, and this next section is a crash course in some of the basics. It is, in simple terms, being aware of your situation.

Predators rely on the weak and vulnerable, whether in the animal kingdom or with humans. Street robbers can recognize a vulnerable potential victim instinctively. The key is not to look like one.

You look vulnerable when you walk down the street using your mobile phone's map feature to find your desired location. The reason is that you are communicating the following:

- You don't know where you are going.

- You don't know where you are, so once they have stolen your phone, you won't be able to contact the police immediately and will probably not know the exact location of the incident. This makes it more difficult for the police to investigate and catch the criminals.
- You are not focused on your surroundings. You are not situationally aware.
- You have at the very least, a phone to steal.

If you stand outside of a London Underground station as it gets dark, you will notice many of the people leaving will open their phones to see whether anyone has been able to live without contacting them over the short journey they have travelled. In doing so, the phone lights up their faces, giving the robbers who hang around near the exit a clear look at their potential prey. They make an immediate assessment of you as a victim. They can tell whether you are a male or a female, young or old, whether they perceive you as someone who will fight back, are alone or are vulnerable. They decide if you are prey!

If you then open the map feature, it's even better. What about calling a friend or putting your headphones on to listen to music to comfort you as you walk home in the dark? Now, you have shut down one of your senses, your hearing… so now you won't hear the attack coming, and you won't have seen the attackers, so you won't be able to give a description.

Being situationally aware means thinking differently from the average person who wanders blindly through their day, oblivious to the threats all around them.

In his excellent book, former US Special Forces expert, Dan Schilling, describes situational awareness as 'knowing where I am and what's around me, what's going on in my surroundings and my place in them'.[97]

Being situationally aware does not mean becoming a Ninja or being obsessed with the idea that an attack is around every corner; it is about being present and thinking ahead. It is about reducing risk.

Being situationally aware is a critical skill everyone should be encouraged to develop. If you are a security professional, it is important to recognize risk and changes to the environment.

Case Study

I was on an advanced 'agent handling' training course in which the instructors deployed surveillance teams to follow the candidates. Our job was to arrange to meet with our 'agents' and then meet them. During the meeting, an exchange had to take place. This all had to be completed without the surveillance teams being able to identify the agent or our meeting place. While waiting at the start point, a local pub, I observed a person who I thought was a member of the surveillance team (who had been given my start point). As we were both waiting, the door opened, and a large individual entered the pub, looked around, bought a coffee and sat in the middle of the pub. After a few minutes, the large individual, having finished his coffee and having had a good look around, left the pub, followed shortly after by the surveillance officer. I left by a different door a short time later and successfully met up with my agent. It turned out that the large individual was, in fact, a well-known local criminal who was so attuned to his local area that he became aware of unusual activity in it, which was me and the surveillance team. He was very situationally aware.

It is vital to be aware of what material you publish on social media. Think about what and when you and your clients publish material. You may be with your clients on an exciting trip or a luxurious holiday when they want to share their experiences with the world. By doing so they may make you, them and their home back in their own country vulnerable. Criminals now know they are not at home, and if they know where they live, this might be a good time to break in and steal their valued possessions and, in doing so, they may engage with you or your colleagues acting as a residential security team.

Case Study

In 2017, ex-England and Chelsea footballer John Terry and his family posted some photos of their skiing holiday on social media. Shortly after the photos appeared online, a gang of professional criminals burgled their home, stealing thousands of pounds worth of personal items, including valuable pieces of jewellery. The couple were extremely distressed by the incident, so much so that they sold the house and moved. But it was completely preventable.[98]

If you are travelling to an important meeting or event, wait until you get home before you post how successful it was. If you are going to an event with live coverage, and your client's attendance will be publicized, think about their home security before you go.

Many prominent people use pseudonyms when booking into a hotel or a restaurant so that they can enjoy the privacy and discretion of being there. Most established venues are used to guests doing this, and so it is rarely an issue. It is best to change the name they use. Otherwise, they get known as 'Donald Duck' everywhere they go, which defeats the object. Doing this can prevent staff from tipping off the paparazzi and ruining your evening.

When out and about, a good practice is to 'horizon scan'. This ensures that you are not caught out by something ahead, such as a large crowd, an angry mob, a fight or a drunk. An interesting exercise to practise as you are walking or driving is to give a commentary on what you see;

this is a practice that all police officers must do when being taught to drive at high speeds and must do when involved in a pursuit. It will surprise you how difficult it can be and how much information you overlook.

As you walk along the street your commentary may sound something like this:

> *Walking towards the centre, a junction 100 metres ahead, two men standing in the doorway smoking, a woman walking towards me with a pram blocking the footpath. At the junction, there are traffic lights. The pedestrian lights are currently on red, with traffic flowing. There is a car parked on the side of the road with a person sitting in the front seat.*

I may not sound like much, but you have identified several potential hazards. Will you have to walk in the road to let the women with the pram pass? Why are the two men standing in the doorway? Is the person in the parked car with them? Should you cross over to the opposite pavement? Is this a potential kidnap situation?

Having some basic body language knowledge can be a huge advantage when being situationally aware. Notice who stands out in an area. What they are doing? Do they look uncomfortable? Are they looking towards an accomplice? Are they wearing a jacket on a hot day? Are they looking restless and fidgeting? None of these examples automatically mean they are a threat, but the fact that you have observed them, and their behaviours, gives you an advantage in assessing them as a threat.

In some cities, moped, scooter and cycle robberies are increasingly common. This is where the rider flies past you and grabs your phone or bag as they do so, stealing your possessions and making off before you have an opportunity to react.

A good tactic, in the first instance, is to walk towards the oncoming traffic so that you can see any approaching vehicles. Second, walk as far away from the road as possible with any bags you or your client are carrying on the building line side of the footpath. That way, if the robbers want to target you, they not only have to mount the pavement – which they will do – but they must come close to the building line, which increases the risk to them. You will see them coming and be better able to avoid their attack. This is situational awareness in action.

These are just a few tips to get you thinking because thinking ahead is the key.

Dan Schilling provides a four-step checklist, which I think is great advice – that is, to consider your surroundings in these four ways, or scenarios.

1. Familiar and safe – eating in your favourite local restaurant.
2. Unfamiliar and safe – eating in a hotel restaurant in a different city.
3. Familiar and unsafe – in a city you know well but where you or your client are clearly foreigners.
4. Unfamiliar and unsafe – in a bar late on the first night of a trip in a city known to be hostile. (See endnote 98 for more details.)

Your situational awareness may be different in each of these scenarios. In scenario 1, 'familiar and safe', you may be more relaxed, let your guard down and miss something obvious because you were not switched on. Equally, in scenario 4, 'unfamiliar and unsafe', while your antenna may be on full alert, you may dismiss a threat as a local cultural practice or be overly reliant on local law enforcement, who may not be trustworthy.

As a security professional, your clients may rely on you to be more situationally aware. This can be exhausting, and mistakes come with tiredness. It may be that the client is more familiar with the surroundings than you are and, for this reason, it may be beneficial to have a briefing before leaving a venue, where you can manage their expectations while ensuring that they identify anything that their situational awareness picks up.

Summary

Situational awareness is a skill that can be improved on. Your level of awareness may depend on your experience, location, and whether you are on or off duty. Being situationally aware can provide an earlier indicator of a threat or a change in the environment that causes you to make a rapid assessment. When you first arrive in a new city or country, it may take some time adjusting to the local environment and understanding what is normal and what is a sign of concern. You may have experienced this during military service overseas or when posted to a new police district – each posing new threats and having a different 'norm'.

It may well be that your clients are more familiar with the locality and people and will recognize something out of place before you do, and their input should be encouraged. Equally, your presence may cause a ripple and attract attention, so being situationally aware of that will be critical and help to reduce your 'situational awareness footprint'.

Chapter 11

Trust your intuition

Introduction

Intuition, from the word 'tuere' meaning 'to guard, to protect'[99] is the ability to understand something without the need for conscious reasoning.

You may know it better as a sixth sense, hunch, gut feeling, business acumen, inspiration or wisdom. It is regarded as an unconscious thought that we haven't rationalized. When you walk into a dark alleyway and see someone walking towards you, you immediately pick up on non-verbal behaviour and assess danger. That is your intuition working. Our intuition is an attribute that, once we learn to listen to and trust, can save our lives. In this section, I share how using your intuition will enhance your safety and impact your decision-making.

Our intuition is different from our instinct in that our intuition tells us something is wrong or different, while our instinct manages our flinch response when someone throws a punch, and we can move or run without thought. In my conversation on personal safety on The Defuse Podcast, Dan Schilling gives a great description of the difference. He uses the example of being in a bar enjoying a social drink when a fight breaks out and you get punched. Your reaction to the punch is when your instincts kick in – your fight or flight. However, *knowing* that a punch is about to be thrown *before* you get hit is down to your observation of the body language and the atmosphere, which tell you something is about to happen. Intuition is what you experience *before* an event, whereas instinct is how you react *after* the event.

As a teenager, I recall being on holiday with friends when we were trying to sneak into a hotel to meet some girls. We couldn't go through the front door – security wouldn't let us in – so my friend suggested we go around the back of the hotel. When we got there, we discovered we had to climb a wall and negotiate a jump of what my friend described as 'a short distance'. It was pitch dark, and some nagging voice was telling me not to jump. I persuaded my friend not to jump, either; it seemed too dangerous.

Thankfully, I listened to my intuition. When we re-visited the site the next day, we found that the jump was about 20 feet, and the drop over the wall was more than 100 feet! We would both have been seriously injured, if not killed.

Ralph Waldo Emerson, the American transcendental philosopher, said 'The primary wisdom is intuition' because it represents a more direct and immediate way of knowing.[100] One of the skills I learned as a police officer was to listen to my 'gut instinct' or my intuition. When dealing with a suspect, or searching dark, suspicious premises, I would draw on my experience to protect myself. This is never more obvious than when a new officer is posted with one who has greater experience. The more experienced officer sees threats earlier, recognizes body language of concern and listens to their inner voice. You can develop this as you, too, listen to your inner voice. This is often experienced when interviewing a victim, who, despite there being little evidence, has an instinctive opinion of who the suspect is, whether it is a former partner or that bloke at the coffee shop, and again, the experienced detective will keep an open mind despite the apparent lack of evidence supporting these views.

Gavin de Becker wrote the book *The Gift of Fear, Survival Signals That Protect Us From Violence* (see endnote 100 for details). In it, he uses the example of Kelly, who, when entering her building, encountered a man offering to help her with her bags. Her intuition was screaming out to her, flagging up numerous warning signs that suggested something was wrong, but as many do, she ignored that inner voice as she didn't want to appear rude. The man subsequently repeatedly raped her, and if it weren't for her quick thinking, he would have killed her, as he had done with other of his victims. He was a serial killer.

This story resonated with me because, as a Scotland Yard detective for 25 of my 30 years in the police, I interviewed many witnesses who told me with the benefit of hindsight, 'There was just something about him/her/them'. Their intuition was flagging up warning signals, which they suppressed.

I am sure you have had similar experiences, having been introduced to someone whom, while you couldn't put your finger on it, you sensed something didn't fit.

Perhaps what they were saying to you, you just knew wasn't true, or maybe it was the way they looked at you or behaved, their body language.

Something unconscious was telling you to run. In the police, I learned to trust my intuition, but many people turn off their inner voice, misunderstanding the signals being communicated or telling themselves to 'give them the benefit of the doubt' or 'be kind; maybe they are just nervous'.

Some of society's highest performers trust and use their intuition. Whether they are sportspeople who just 'instinctively' know where their teammate will be on the field to receive their pass or businesspeople who trust their 'gut' when making decisions, these people appear to be more in tune with their surroundings and at ease.

Dr Wong has suggested there are seven different types of intuition. For the purpose of our self-protection, he refers to our primitive instincts. He describes this as self-preservation, such as the flight-or-fight syndrome, avoidance responses, pleasure-seeking, and instinctive responses to reduce primary needs, such as food, water, and safety. (Refer back to endnote 101 for details.)

Case Study

In 2004, Clare Bernal thought she had found her dream job working at a beauty counter at Harvey Nichols in Knightsbridge, London. It was while she was at work that she met Michael Pech. Shortly after joining the store as a security guard, Pech asked Clare for a date.

They went on three dates in three weeks. However, it quickly became apparent that he was extremely possessive and obsessed with her. Clare listened to her intuition and finished the relationship. His behaviour escalated, and in due course, he was sacked from his job and convicted of harassing her. Unfortunately, others failed to recognize his threat, and he was released on bail.

On 13 September 2005, while on bail awaiting sentencing, Pech walked into Harvey Nicholls, approached Clare from behind, and shot her four times, killing her. He then shot himself dead.[101]

When a stranger approaches you in a car park and offers to help you with your shopping, what is your inner voice telling you? What about when a new person appears at the gates outside your children's school? How about when you are out at a bar with a friend, and a person approaches you at the bar and engages you in conversation? You and your friend catch each other's eye, and a mutual understanding is agreed upon: 'Drink up. We're leaving!'

How often do you watch the news of a horrific incident such as a murder and listen to the witnesses telling the reporter, 'There was always something about him/her/them'? Why are we prepared to listen to the nagging voice in hindsight but not in real time?

Too often, we shut down and suppress our inner voice for fear of being rude, unsociable or any number of other excuses.

We have intuition for a reason: to keep us safe. It is an inbuilt skill, not something we must input. Listening to it lets us fine-tune our skills and learn to use them more effectively.

Summary

We are all born with intuition; some just learn to listen to it better. Luckily, it is a skill that can be developed and relied upon. Our intuition is an unconscious process that constantly scans for threats and is designed to keep us safe. Far too many people either fail to listen or turn down their intuition for fear of upsetting or being rude to others. In the same way that we can instantly feel a connection with someone, we can also feel that someone poses a threat or a risk to us. Phrases such as 'gut feeling' and 'I can feel it my bones' are entrenched in our language and have existed for eternity. Victims of crime often say, 'There was just something about him/her/them'. If only they had listened to their intuition, they may not have been a victim. Many successful people have suggested that listening to their inner voice (intuition) was the secret to their success. As a security professional, you should have your intuition turned on, turned up and listened to it. It is your first line of defence and the one that always has your best interest in mind.

Chapter 12

Personal safety

Introduction

In this chapter, I will cover some of the key elements of how you can feel safer, including some unconscious skills. Harnessing these skills will help you to feel safer. Some excellent work has been done on personal safety with a specific focus on the safety of women and children. Your clients may well feel exposed and apprehensive about travelling on public transport, never quite knowing whether the person who has suddenly recognized them is a friend or a foe.

By the end of this chapter, your personal arsenal of tools for feeling safer will be significantly enhanced and you will be better placed to share these skills with those you protect.

What is personal safety?

Personal safety is a key skill that you might think should be taught in schools, colleges and universities. However, that is far from reality. The truth is that most of the population has never had any training, and there is no officially recognized training. Police officers are often tasked with delivering personal safety training, yet most have never had specific training. Some of what they teach may fall into other categories, such as conflict resolution. In an earlier life, I was a 'police officer safety trainer', and when I look at current courses being promoted as personal safety training by the police, it appears to me that they are nothing short of a re-branding exercise and are not what they appear to be.

One reputable organization described personal safety as 'An individual's ability to go about their everyday life free from the threat or fear of psychological, emotional or physical harm from others.'

Your personal safety is your responsibility. Personal safety is also context-driven. There are issues of lone worker safety, travel safety, female safety, night-time economy safety, and more.

The irony is that in the current surveillance culture, where you cannot move without being monitored by CCTV in some cities, many people feel less safe. Whether that is because of the reality or because of their perception is up for debate; however, knife crime is increasing and rarely a day goes by when we don't hear a dreadful story about someone being randomly attacked or killed.

The UK Office of National Statistics published a report in 2022 on Perceptions of Personal Safety and Experiences of Harassment, providing an interesting insight.[102] It concluded the following:

- People felt less safe walking alone in all settings after dark than during the day, with women feeling less safe than men after dark
- Disabled people felt less safe in all settings than non-disabled people.
- More women (27%) than men (16%) reported they had experienced at least one form of harassment in the previous 12 months.

Some of the findings might be obvious, such as feeling less safe after dark. However, there is no doubt that women are feeling less safe and, because of recent events, many feel they cannot trust the police to keep them safe either.

There is plenty of guidance on the market to help people feel safer. However, some of that advice suggests people break the law by carrying weapons and other implements. Others have offered advice about safety in hotels and advised using door jams and other devices. There is an argument that despite such tools breaching Health and Safety guidance, the benefits outweigh the risks associated. As ever, it is a personal choice.

Whatever action you decide to take to feel safer must not make you less safe. Drinking alcohol to give you courage or taking drugs to diminish your insecurities rarely works.

Alcohol and drugs are key drivers in personal safety for two reasons. First, where you find alcohol and drugs are being consumed, the greater the likelihood you will encounter aggressive and violent behaviour. Second, your ability to make rational decisions and choices is diminished should you choose to consume either.

So, how do you keep yourself safe?

Mindful of the previous paragraph, it is best to limit your alcohol consumption and avoid drugs, which in almost every case are illegal and hence require you to compromise yourself to purchase or acquire them. If you see someone who is clearly drunk or otherwise inebriated by some other form of substance, avoid them.

Wherever possible, avoid conflict. In almost every case of robbery, for example, you will be safer to hand over whatever the thief asks for than engage in a heated dispute and get involved in a fight. Most robbers, even those visibly armed, want your possessions. They do not want to hurt you, but they will if they must, and they will if the encounter gets physical. Put simply, nothing you own is worth more than your life or the life of a loved one.

Should you be confronted by a person hell-bent on getting into a confrontation, a good strategy is to hold your arms up, bent at the elbow. This can be seen as a submissive posture, but it also unconsciously communicates that you are not a threat to them. Do everything you can to be non-threatening. I was taught this hugely effective technique as a young policeman in London, and it has worked almost every time I have used it.

If a person is ranting, rather than get into an argument, let them carry on ranting. When they have finished, ask them if they have finished. If they haven't, let them carry on until they *have* finished. In almost every case, they will eventually run out of steam, and once they realize they cannot get a rise out of you, they tend to quit. If you have ever been told to 'calm down', you'll know that it tends to have the opposite effect, so think about the words you use.

It is better to walk away and let the other person believe they are right than compromise your own safety to prove to yourself that you are the smarter or more intelligent person.

Much of personal safety is common sense, such as not openly carrying or publicly counting wads of cash. The previous chapters on situational awareness and intuition are critical factors in personal safety.

Here are ten random tips to keep you and your clients safe (and yes… I know some are obvious, but they are worth repeating!).

1. Be aware of where you are and how vulnerable you are.
2. Do not carry your phone or wallet in your back pocket.
3. If you are being followed or are confronted, turn to face the person because most attacks come from behind. Shout, use a panic alarm and draw attention to your situation.
4. Have your car keys in your hand so you don't have to linger before entering your car.
5. Check the interior of your vehicle for intruders before entering your car.

6. Keep the office door locked if you work alone or after business hours.
7. Change your Wi-Fi password at home, and don't log on to open networks when you are out.
8. Before a long trip, make sure your vehicle is in good condition.
9. Choose your hotel with care. Go for one with good reviews and security, and when you arrive, familiarize yourself with the location of fire extinguishers, fire exits, assembly points and evacuation routes.
10. When travelling abroad, find the emergency number before leaving home and programme it into your phone.

Summary

Your personal safety is your responsibility. Alcohol and drugs reduce people's ability to keep themselves safe and increase the risk to others. Where possible, avoid venues where drugs and alcohol are consumed.

Being prepared before any journey, no matter how familiar, is a key factor, as is listening to your intuition. If you feel unsafe leaving work late at night, leave earlier or lock the doors if you must stay late.

If you are confronted by criminals in the street, give them your possessions, if that is what they want; it is not worth risking your safety for the sake of a replaceable item.

Wherever possible, avoid getting into an argument or confrontation. It is better to be agreeable and walk away than to feel like you must be right and end up injured.

Before any trip, ensure your vehicle is in good condition, and if staying in a hotel, be mindful that you often get what you pay for. It is sensible to ensure that where you are staying is safe and that you are familiar with the emergency drills and numbers if you are abroad.

Chapter 13

Stop giving away your secrets

Introduction

We now live in a digital age where almost everything exists online. While that has plenty of benefits, it also presents risks. In the modern world, many of our bills, banking, identities and social life are managed online, and data is now a key commodity. Almost every time you go online, someone tries to acquire your data, whether by asking or assuming you wish to subscribe to a newsletter or inviting you to enter your details to win a prize. Banking, once the bastion of the local community, is now almost non-existent in real terms. There is an assumption that everyone is online. The volume of our private data that others store and share is beyond our comprehension. This chapter will discuss this subject from a risk perspective and provide some guidance on how we can reduce the potential harm that is caused daily.

Privacy and public relations

Public relations (PR) refer to managing how others see and feel about a person, brand or company. It is essential to business, branding and the celebrity world. What it doesn't mean, nor should it do, is put the person or organization being promoted at increased risk.

PR teams rarely engage with any security or threat functions that a business or prominent person has, and yet they should do. There are several reasons for this.

When considering the safety of a prominent person, one of the key areas of risk is predictability. Very often, they can be employed to promote an event, or their presence is expected to support a cause or a friend. These social and business events are often promoted, and therefore, any person seeking to cause harm, or any fixated person, will know where and when they will be at any specific time. The security at the event and the person's personal team, should they have one, will need to know that there has been publicity and potential security risks because of that publicity. They can then be prepared for those issues and ensure that unwanted people can be prevented from attending and disrupting the event.

Second, the presence of a prominent person at a specific location highlights the presence of goods such as expensive jewellery and other items of value, which may require additional security.

In my previous career in the Metropolitan Police, I was employed as a counter-terrorist security coordinator. My role was to advise on, plan and coordinate the security elements of large-scale or significant policing operations and events, including those of the Royal Family, Government, or the military. A key element of the planning phase was understanding the media strategy. This enabled me to know what information the media team was planning to release and whether or how an adversary might benefit from using that information.

Case Study

In 2016, reality star Kim Kardashian announced to the world that she was in Paris, France, with an Instagram post stating simply 'Parisian Vibes'. She was followed by the paparazzi from the airport to her hotel – a private residence transformed into a luxurious guesthouse. It is also known as having very lax security. Because of the discretion required by their exclusive guests, there is no CCTV camera. The door entry code was well known because it hadn't changed in years. It was a prime target for what is known as home-jacking – robbing wealthy people in their homes.

Kardashian was followed everywhere she went by an entourage of paparazzi, which may also have provided opportunities for hostile reconnaissance to be conducted. This is the process of following and watching someone or somewhere for the purpose of learning about their security and identifying the vulnerabilities.

Kardashian posted Instagram photos from Paris. The one posted the day after her arrival was an apparent selfie of her with some of her jewellery. The photo showed her with diamonds in her mouth and a 20-carat diamond ring on her finger. Her then-husband Kanye West had apparently purchased the ring in New York for around US$4 million. Kim signed the post with three blue diamond emojis.

These posts were gold dust for potential thieves and those targeting her.

At about 2:30am, a gang entered the hotel. After securing the night porter, they went directly to Kardashian's room. Having broken into it, they held Kardashian at gunpoint and tied her hands together. Then they locked her in a bathroom. During the incident, she genuinely feared she was going to be killed and begged for her life.

All because she overshared information that put her at risk.

The thieves – many of whom were over 60 years of age and dubbed the 'grandpa gangsters' by social media – were subsequently convicted and sentenced to prison terms. One of them, Yunis Abbas, later stated: 'Since she was throwing money away, I was there to collect it, and that was that. Guilty? No, I don't care.'

Of those who flaunt their wealth online, he said: 'They should be a little less showy towards people who can't afford it. For some people, it's provocative.'[103]

Other celebrities have been put at risk by their PR when they have effectively published their home address and showed off their valuables when appearing in online articles or magazines. It is clear from these exposures that no one considered the risks of such oversharing. As a security professional, you should be aware of any publicity that your client has planned. This will enable you to advise whether it might have security implications and therefore plan for any unwanted attention, and be mindful that your own personal safety may be at enhanced risk.

Ailsa Anderson, former head of communications for Queen Elizabeth II, told me when being interviewed for my podcast that even though members of the UK Royal Family might have a documentary crew following them around for months at a time, nothing was ever allowed to be broadcast or published until it has passed a security review to ensure nothing was revealed by accident. This is good practice.

Oversharing can also occur unwittingly by posting selfies unaware of what the image reveals.

Case Study

A wealthy client, concerned that he was overexposed, requested I audit him and his family.

In the audit, we quickly identified that his teenage daughter was very active on social media and revealed far too much. When I presented our findings to him, I revealed that I had identified a particular artwork on display in his living room. The painting was valued at more than £6 million and, having no doubt that it was an original, a contact of mine suggested that a private buyer could be found and would pay well for that stolen painting. I also found his home's plans on the internet and, as such, could plot exactly which room the painting was in and how to access that room. Also available online were the plans of the extensions he had built, with the positions of his security cameras. He and his wife were active on the London social scene, and details of events they were due to attend were often published in advance, allowing me an insight into when the property might be empty. All publicly available information would enable me to plan a high-value burglary and may have significant implications on a subsequent insurance claim. As a result of this information being available, we conducted a full security review. We removed harmful material where possible and installed additional security where appropriate.

Organizations do the same. Many government buildings, art galleries, plus other buildings and events of interest, overshare. Their websites reveal plans of the buildings and emergency rendezvous, which can then be targeted. It is far easier to initiate a bomb scare or a fire alarm, empty a building to a pre-planned rendezvous point, and then attack that venue than it is to smuggle weapons or explosives into a secure building.

Many of these same organizations provide guided tours of their buildings with inadequately briefed guides who, when asked, will reveal details that tourists don't need to know, thereby compromising security.

Data brokers and hackers sell our personal, identifiable and private information daily, often on the deep and dark web. This enables others to acquire our data, create fake profiles, commit identity theft, and target us for crime. While I am an advocate of good cyber security, we must recognize that despite the very best systems that may keep us safe from unwanted intrusions, hackers are targeting global brands, and that is how they acquire our data. No matter how good you think your cyber security systems are, your data and your client's data are being sold. A regular check or, even better, monitoring of your data can provide reassurance and increase privacy and security. The data that is being repurposed can then be removed every 24 hours.

Social media

Social media is a significant factor in the success of some people's personal or corporate brands, a place that you may visit to keep up to date with the latest news and gossip or perhaps to learn a new skill. For some, it is a hugely positive experience. For others, it is a toxic culture full of hate, abuse and hostility, encouraging suicide and even murder. So, how do we keep ourselves and loved ones safe when using social media? In this section, I will share some simple tips to consider when abused or threatened, subject to unpleasant or hostile comments, or when you feel that you are being targeted or stalked by a known or unknown party.

Social media is neither good nor bad; it is the people who use it, and some would argue, manage it, that are responsible. It can be an echo chamber and, for some, a place where conspiracy theories and extremist views are shared and where the vulnerable are groomed. There is no question that it has been a channel for extremists, be they terrorists or others driven by views outside the parameters of what the majority would consider acceptable to recruit, conspire and collaborate.

Alongside the social media debate runs the equally misinformed conversation about the issue of anonymity. Some users are indeed completely anonymous, but not as many as some would have you believe. The problem with the arguments about anonymity is that social media is a global community, and many would be unable to exist on social media, let alone express their views, share witness accounts of wrongdoing, or engage with communities banned where they live, such as the LGBTQ+ communities. It would not be possible for the UK to enforce compulsory IDs for all users, while expecting countries in which human rights are ignored not to do the same. Equally, a good deal of the abuse and threats received by UK-based politicians and footballers emanates from abroad. How would the UK Government advise that it is policed? To be clear, I am not suggesting that the social media platforms themselves shouldn't take greater responsibility, but that is a discussion for another book.

When using social media, one of the key pieces of advice is to protect your personal information. Far too often, people overshare on social media. From a commercial perspective, social media's main purpose is to gather your data. That data is then sold, shared or used to market and sell to you. When you are researching buying a new fridge online, have you ever noticed which ads suddenly appear on your news feed?

By researching individuals using open source and social media, I have found priceless artefacts they possess, what schools their children go to, when they are on holiday, which gym they visit at the same time each day, where they work and who they are dating (possibly even while they are married). All this information is revealed by posts, selfies, the information logged, and other people posting and tagging you in.

If you are using social media for both business and pleasure, separate the two. If that means you have two accounts on each platform you use, so be it.

If you are abused, threatened, or intimidated by someone on social media, the following is good advice:

1. Screenshot the post/image. This is especially relevant on 'X'/ Twitter as once a post or profile is deleted, they will insist it cannot be retrieved.

2. Never respond. By doing so you open your network up to the person targeting you, who probably only has a few followers.

3. Understand and be familiar with the platform's terms and conditions and their reporting policies.

4. Report them to the platform. If they don't know about it, they will unlikely do anything.

5. Report them to the police if you feel suitably aggrieved.

6. Mute, don't block. Muting is better so that you can, as required, track any escalation of behaviour or threats and evidence their behaviour.

7. If your client is being targeted, ensure they share their experience with friends. This is especially important if they are being harassed or stalked. Sharing how they feel and keeping a record of what is happening and how it makes them feel is good evidence in the event of any law enforcement investigation. Telling others is good practice so they are aware in the event of being contacted by the person.

8. If you see a post that upsets, angers, offends or annoys you or your clients, report it. Third-party reporting is welcomed, and evidentially, it can be hugely impactful. You don't have to be the recipient.

9. Everyone has their own tipping point. If being on social media is getting too much for you or your clients, you can pause, delete, switch off. You do not have to stay.

10. Review the online settings regularly as they change. Ensure you are not sharing your location or other key information. If your social media is on your phone, you must check both the phone and your app's settings.

11. Don't take it personally (easier said than done, I know). In my experience of investigating thousands of cases, they usually emanate from individuals who envy your success, looks, wealth or whatever else it is they are commenting on. They don't deserve any attention or a response.

Summary

In this chapter, I have addressed the issue of how much of our private data is publicly available and how this can make us all feel less safe. The subject of PR and the associated risks of such activity, not considering the security risks of publishing material to promote prominent people or events, was highlighted with the infamous Kardashian robbery in Paris used to illustrate the point. Other cases have involved celebrities inviting magazines and other media into their homes, who then publish images of the home, including some priceless assets together with details that make identifying the location easier than it should be. It is hard to exist as a prominent person without a social media presence, and even if they are careful what they post, it is important to understand what is being posted by other family members, colleagues and friends. Historical material posted, perhaps even before they were in the public eye, can be re-surfaced and be used against them with what might have been appropriate some years ago, now failing the politically correct test and causing significant reputational harm and, worst-case scenario, being cancelled. Finally, I address the subject of social engineering, cybercrime, and data breaches. This is where the previously discussed issues are then used against your clients by criminals and other adversaries. It is a hugely profitable business; however, it can be thwarted by some simple good practices and continued training and refreshing. A service that delivers real results is the monitoring of your PII data, which is currently being made available on the internet, deep web, and the web.

Chapter 14

Complacency kills

Introduction

In this section, I will discuss how complacency is the greatest threat to personal safety. From our most basic daily practices to our politicians' safety, becoming complacent will undermine every piece of good practice. I will use examples of how complacency contributed to security failures, including fatal attacks, to demonstrate the importance of this critical element.

The very best security policy is only as good as its constant implementation.

Being safer requires personal responsibility, if you have a security team tasked with keeping your clients safe, each member of that team has individual responsibility. Being safe requires proactivity. Much like other areas of life, being ahead of the game is better. That means that you have a degree of control. The alternative is that you are in constant crisis, which is stressful, expensive, and harmful. Being safe and protecting people and assets requires a professional approach. This chapter will detail how that is achieved.

Be proactive

Throughout this book, I have referred to being proactive in several areas, and there is a very good reason for that. In personal safety, people often act after something bad has happened. In this section, I hope to encourage you to change that and be proactive.

As any successful person will know, being proactive is the key to their success. I can guarantee that the one thing that no successful person does is sit around waiting for business to come to them. A key element is their proactivity, their get-up-and-go. The Scout's motto 'Be prepared' demands a mindset of proactivity. A great friend and mentor had a saying, 'If it's to be, it's up to me.'

Looking after your personal security and safety is the same; proactive people are more successful at staying safe.

Despite this being the case, many of my clients come to me when a crisis has occurred. A third party is targeting them and they are concerned about their safety. By the time this has happened, it is likely that that third party will already have researched the client and potentially identified several vulnerabilities. Conducting a vulnerability assessment and then ascertaining where these gaps are is usual. The problem is that I cannot make the third party forget what they are now aware of. What I can then do is implement various options to mitigate the identified vulnerabilities. This all comes at an additional cost, which they would have likely avoided had they come to me before the crisis arose.

Case Study

A female CEO of a large brand approached us following several concerning messages she received. Understandably, she was concerned about identifying who the person was and whether she was in danger. Our assessment identified that her home address was visible, as were her home plans, the details of which school her children attended, and even the gym she attended on a regular basis. We were able to tidy up her digital footprint. However, we couldn't tell whether the anonymous person harassing her had already identified the same information. Due to her profile and the fear and anxiety this incident caused her, she requested that we provide additional security protection for her until such time as we were able to make her feel safer. Additional security is invasive and costly, but that was a necessity for our client.

Had this investigation into her vulnerability been completed when she first took on her new role, and the relevant steps taken to anonymize her while monitoring for any further leaks of information, it would have been less expensive and saved her the anxiety and fear she experienced. We subsequently identified that the person of concern was not based in the same country, and our profiling suggested that they were attention-seeking rather than posing a threat, but the experience was sufficient for the client to request that we work with her to improve her personal safety and monitor her to alert her of any emerging issues.

A lesson can be learned from the aviation industry, which has an aviation safety management system that has three functions:[104]

- Identify precursors that lead to risk.
- Identify threats before they become dangerous.
- Understand what behaviours and attitudes are influencing safety performance.

In essence, these three objectives are what proactivity does. This applies whether you are considering installing a security system – hopefully, before the client is burgled – conducting situational awareness, or having a digital vulnerability audit.

The reality is that, regardless of the context, being proactive will save you money and prevent anxiety and reputational harm, and yet so many still have a reactive mindset, especially when it comes to themselves.

Complacency creates a false sense of security, which is critical when deployed in high-risk environments. When I was first deployed to Northern Ireland, my focus was understandably high. The key was to maintain that level of focus throughout the deployment, which required effort as I became comfortable with the level of risk.

With complacency, you risk making assumptions. You assume that you are managing the risk. In 1984, the day after the IRA bombed the hotel that then Prime Minister Margaret Thatcher and the Conservative Party were staying in, the IRA released a statement: 'Today we were unlucky, but remember we only have to be lucky once. You will have to be lucky always.'[105] That is where targeting a complacency comes in, waiting for the target to slip up!

When I set up the investigative team in Parliament following the murder of Jo Cox MP, one challenge I faced was persuading MPs to take up the security measures that were available to them. This challenge was simplified every time a security incident was directed at an MP. At this point, there would be a rush to secure the measures available. Once the dust had settled, complacency would again set in, and the demand for the security measures would slow down again. It is easy to become complacent and forget to maintain security standards without daily threats.

I recently met with a Member of Parliament after a request to visit their constituency office to discuss wider security issues. Having been invited into their office and I asked them whether the seating plan was how they met their other visitors. It was clear to me that the advice provided was not being followed.

This complacency is also apparent in the commercial sector. I have always believed that proactive action is better than reactive action.

One of my key recommendations for any public or prominent figure is to have their online vulnerability reviewed regularly. As has been previously referred to in this book, this review seeks to identify what private data is publicly available. I often conduct these on our clients when a crisis occurs, and I'm tasked with investigating. I believe these should be conducted regularly because data is constantly being acquired and published on the dark web as breach data. Equally, it is not unusual that family members, children and friends unintentionally reveal private information or post images that you'd prefer they hadn't.

This same complacency is present in most vetting or due diligence processes. A failure to conduct a proper vetting process and to repeat it is regularly one of the key issues in a failure to recognize an insider threat. Very often, due diligence is little more than a box-ticking exercise, confirming what is already known. However, any due diligence or vetting process is only a snapshot in time. The excuse is often the cost of having a proper process, which involves a regular or random process repeat. This is compounded when hiring 'external' workers on more flexible contracts accompanied by a reduction in the pre-employment scrutiny in conducting the required vetting. (Refer back to endnote 50 for more details on a publication titled *Better Safe Than Sorry*.)

The excuse of cost must be balanced against the average cost of an insider threat, which can run into millions of pounds.[106] A regular review is good practice, so here are a few 'reminder' questions to consider:

- Has a digital vulnerability audit been conducted recently?
- Have passwords been changed recently?
- Has a security survey been conducted at home or at work?
- Has the setting of any mobile phones, tablets, and laptops been checked recently?
- Have social media profile settings been checked to ensure they are correct?
- Have children and their teachers been briefed on what to do if their parents or carers are late or unable to pick them up from school? Remember, teachers change so conducting a regular review is a good idea.

- Have locks or W-Fi codes been changed recently, especially when moving to a new property, or when someone moves out?
- Have vehicle you use had an annual service to ensure everything works as it should?
- Have you had a regular health or dentist check-up recently?

Summary

Complacency is the security professional's greatest threat.

Whether that is your complacency or that of your clients. As the IRA state when they spoke for all terrorists and criminals, they only have to get lucky once, and they rely on our complacency to get lucky.

Self-discipline is the antidote to personal complacency and is the foundations of any military unit's success. Contrary to what those who have never served think, the military teach their soldiers to be self-disciplined. Should a soldier become complacent and lack the required self-discipline, it will be enforced on to them.

A security regime or programme is only as good as the time it was last checked. Complacency can damage security fences and prevent CCTV from functioning properly, as well as failing to properly brief and debrief colleagues working with us.

Having a system of constant and regular review prevents such occurrences. This relates to the maintenance of our health and our vehicles. Ensuring that our vehicles are regularly serviced, that the tyres are properly inflated, and that the oil is topped up ensures that they are running efficiently and less susceptible to breakdown.

Complacency kills.

Chapter 15

The security profession

Introduction

The security industry is a growing global giant. A huge number and variety of individuals and companies are now involved in it. In this next subject, I am going to share my personal, completely biased views on the industry, some of the issues and concerns, and how to find a suitable professional when you have that need.

Several UK professional associations, groups, and authorities seek to attract members and highlight themselves as industry leaders. I know some, but not all, of these professional bodies and have been a member of a few at some point. As ever, some are better than others. Some focus on specialist areas of the industry, while others are generalists.

The Security Industry Authority is a UK Government organization and defines its role as 'monitoring the activities of people operating within the private security industry and taking enforcement action where necessary, setting, and approving standards of conduct and training for the private security industry. It recommends ways to improve standards in the private security industry'.[107] This definition is not entirely accurate as they only really have any authority over specific areas of the industry that require a license to operate, train or sell certain activities.

In essence, these are public-facing roles where those involved are required to have licences to operate. This captures a small percentage of the industry and, as an example, doesn't include me.

A few international professional associations, such as ASIS and The Association of European Threat Assessment Professionals (AETAP) also provide industry-standard training together with the sister organizations covering the rest of the world. These organizations include ATAP in the US, APATAP in the Asia-Pacific region, CATAP in Canada, AfATAP in Africa and ALATAP covering Latin America.

As in any industry, some of these organizations are very good at raising standards, others are less effective, and many are considered nothing more than a box-ticking money-making scheme. My personal experience of the industry is that there are some exceptional individuals and companies, and a significant number of charlatans and snake oil salespeople.

So, mindful of the lack of international standards and accreditation, how do you identify professionals whom you can trust and rely upon to act professionally?

Experience is a huge factor in any industry; however, this is a crucial element within the security industry. You may have exceptional credentials, first-class academic qualifications, and a very fancy website, but unless you have the experience to match all of those, they will mean very little.

The security industry includes former law enforcement, military, and government employees. While they undoubtedly have unique skill sets and experiences, you don't have to have been employed in any of those fields to be excellent in the security industry. Increasingly, more women and people of different cultures and communities are joining the industry, which can only be positive. Like any industry, diversity makes it stronger, and while they may initially lack the experience of others, given the opportunities, those who are good will prove their worth.

Throughout this book, I have used case studies to help bring to life the lessons I have shared. While they may give a snapshot into the types of cases and results a professional may have engaged in, they are just that – a snapshot.

Most of my clients come via referrals. The referrals are made by former clients, intermediaries or partners such as lawyers, wealth managers and business colleagues. Equally, when I am looking for a professional, whether it be an electrician, estate agent or a dentist, I ask my network who they would recommend. I have accrued a well-vetted network of professionals within my eco-system so that while I focus on my specialism, I can draw upon the expertise of those I know, like and trust. My network is international, and this has helped clients enormously when they have multi-jurisdictional issues or whether they are travelling and require someone they trust in some of the more dangerous parts of the world.

Case Study

A client was travelling to South America to close a deal, and due to the location and the nature of his business, they wanted to have some discreet protection. They asked me whether I could help. Within an hour, I had secured the help of a vetted and trusted operative with local knowledge, who spoke both English and the local language, and was able to provide his own team to help my client feel safer. Before my client left the UK, I was able to introduce them to each other, arrange a Zoom call, and build some initial rapport. The operative was able to advise which hotel to stay in, routes to be used and even restaurants to eat at. My client enjoyed a successful trip and was hugely impressed by the support they received while in the country.

A word of caution when employing individuals to provide protection or guarding services: increasingly, there has been something of a 'race to the bottom' based purely on fees. It is known that some companies fill these roles by sending out a post on a WhatsApp group and effectively filling 'bums on seats'. This is a hugely unprofessional and dangerous trend. This is where doing your homework is critical, ensuring that those you engage conduct proper vetting, brief and de-brief, and pay their staff properly. They are there to look after your safety; the least you'd expect is that they take that seriously.

The security profession can be divided into employed and self-employed or consultants and advisers. Some, me included, have become Chartered Security Professionals and have the post-nominals of CSyP. At the time of writing, there are fewer than 300 Chartered Security Professionals globally, although it is a predominantly UK-based organization. Becoming a Chartered Security Professional is a means of being recognized and continuing to represent the highest standards and ongoing proficiency. It is the gold standard of competence in security.

Approximately 262,800 security industry employees are estimated to work in the United Kingdom.[108] None of us is an expert in everything. While some are generalists, others operate in specific niches; these include technical, physical and academic subjects. Those employed include front-line security guards to experts in nuclear security and pretty much everything in between.

At its best, the security profession is a community that works together, recognizing that we are lucky enough to have some of the most talented specialists within our midst. I'd like to think that we are all part of a jigsaw puzzle, and collectively, we can solve any problem.

The SAFER Model® process

To conclude the book, I am going to walk you through one the investigative processes that I use. The SAFER Model® takes a client away from the problem being presented, enabling a full investigation and resolution, and including looking after any psychological harm caused.

The SAFER Model' is a five-phase process that follows the threat assessment model of identifying, assessing, and managing any investigation where threats are made, or risks exist. Much like any model, it is flexible providing a structure for a professionally managed investigation.

Figure 15.1: The SAFER Model®

Strategize investigation

The first phase is the strategy phase. This is a critical phase, as it ensures we understand the problem that our client is facing and the outcome they want. What is critical is to understand the scope at this early stage and avoid over promising on what can be delivered. We want to ensure that our clients have the very best service they can have, achieve realistic results and understand the timescales for achieving that. During this phase we ensure our client is aware what material we will require from them to achieve the agreed outcomes, and whether we are conducting a phased approach or a standalone piece of work. We will work with our clients to understand who else needs to be involved, what information they have or level of involvement they have. As an example, they may want to include or exclude someone from being involved, such as their agent or management team. The issue we are working with to resolve may be very personal or it might be business related. Once we have agreed to strategy, we can commence the investigation.

Analyse facts and identify risks

This is the initial phase of the investigation, where we establish what evidence exists. This may be sourced by a digital investigation, a vulnerability assessment or from existing evidence from our client such as letters, emails or other documentation.

Once we have gathered the available evidence we conduct an analysis, to establish the level of risk, whether specific thresholds have been met which may include criminal or civil burdens of proof and where we have conducted a scoping exercise, whether we have established sufficient evidence to continue with the investigation and where we might focus our enquiries.

Forensic assessment

The assessment phase takes the evidence that has been seized and then compares that to other processes to understand what that information means. Several different tools can be used, and they are often known as Structured Professional Judgement (SPJ) tools. These are an evidence-based approach that combines empirically validated tools with professional judgement and can used by anyone once trained. Without using an SPJ, you are, in essence, guessing based on your experiences.

When using an SPJ, it is critical to understand how they have been verified and under what circumstances. Culture is key in these assessment tools, especially when indigenous populations are involved. This is because different cultures may have different rules. For example, you may distrust someone who fails to maintain eye contact during a conversation until you realize that in their culture, it is disrespectful to do so, hence why they don't. If an SPJ has excluded specific cultures when researched, its use may be prejudiced. This may cause an issue if used to decide before a person is dismissed from work for their behaviour, and the decision was used based on an SPJ that has excluded specific groups that the individual is part of.

Forensic assessment may include a referral to one of our experienced Clinical and Forensic Psychologists who will review the available material and make an assessment. It is a key service that we deliver. The various profiles that we conduct can identify risk, personality traits and stalking typologies, and help to design a communication and engagement programme or a safety plan designed to reduce harm to both the client and the person of concern who may be suffering from a mental illness and require careful engagement to prevent escalating any issues presented. This is a specialist service and part of the model that requires professional attention, and any advice provided will take the context into account and again refer to the science behind the decision-making and assessment.

In simple terms we ask the question: 'So what?' What does this mean for you? How can you use the assessment? Is it relevant to you? This evaluation then provides options for managing the threats or risks identified.

Engage and liaise

Once we have established what material or evidence is available and what the level of risk is, we can begin to engage and liaise with other stakeholders. This may include us engaging with contacts that we have at social media platforms or other relevant organisations, with lawyers, law enforcement and other identified and relevant parties.

Using our contacts in specific organizations can significantly reduce the response time and increase the likelihood of a positive outcome.

The purpose may be to gather further information, to request that information is removed, request legal advice or representation, or to engage with law enforcement.

One of the key roles we provide when representing clients is to engage with law enforcement on their behalf or act as an independent stalking advocate. This is to provide safety planning as part of a risk-lead service. It is quite normal when engaging with the police as a victim, that the service you receive is less than expected. The terminology used can be confusing and at times the advice provided in incorrect or outdated.

Our expertise in countering stalking and unwanted attention in general enables us to ensure that you receive the very best service, and we can act as your representatives, as a bridge between you and the police ensuring that the information you receive is accurate, ands relevant. The impact of this has been proven to reduce the stress and anxiety involved and to help achieve better results.

Risk management and reassure

Risk management is a critical phase. It is a fact that the stalking risk assessment process used by many UK police is outdated and flawed. Throughout this book, we have discussed the importance of understanding what risk management is, and how to implement it. Understanding the level of risk and the proportionate measures that will mitigate the identified risks is a critical element of helping our clients feel safer.

Once the information is researched, seized, and assessed, and the application is forensically analysed and evaluated, we must do something. We need to resolve the issue presented that initiated this process. This is discussed with the client. Once the options are presented, we discuss how to resolve the issue.

This may involve:

- conducting civil legal procedures
- target hardening the premises or person
- moving the person threatened
- monitoring data and activities on the internet and deep and dark web
- dismissing the person of concern from their employment where relevant
- conducting a thorough security review and tidying the digital footprint of the client.

As we have discussed in this book, being subjected to unwanted attention, abuse, threats or other targeting can, and very often does, have a significant impact on those affected. The feeling of being unsafe can cause paranoia, hypervigilance and a decline in mental health. During this final phase, we seek to resolve those issues. The plan may be to refer to a specialist who might provide therapeutic support, additional physical or protective security or close protection, depending on the requirements.

Our Family Liaison service is a service we provide that can be of benefit to our clients both in the UK or abroad when a traumatic or critical incident occurs. Delivered by a former Counter Terrorist Family Liaison expert, previously deployed internationally to support British citizens following a traumatic incident, this specialist service provides expert assistance and guidance during or following an incident of concern. The expertise and knowledge of dealing with the emotional and practical issues following a trauma are invaluable, especially in the case of a death, serious injury or other traumatic occurrences towards a loved one. We pride ourselves on our ability to provide this level of practical support, including repatriation and liaison with authorities, while also addressing the clients holistic needs.

Summary

The security profession is a hugely diverse community. It now benefits from a huge variant of experiences and niches, supported by operational experts and serious academics. Understanding more about the security industry, albeit primarily in the UK, may help you to choose where you fit into the community and how you want your career to develop. Being a member of an industry organization does not mean an individual or provider is better, albeit some roles require licences. I'm a great believer in referrals, and because I don't pretend to know or do it all, I rely on trusted partners to refer clients worldwide.

The final element is an introduction to the model that we use at Defuse Global. As in many professions, there are those who have spent years honing their skills and those who have been on a course. Our model requires operational expertise in each area. There are those who have been on an open-source course, and then there are those who have spent years working with the government or law enforcement and have real-world expertise of not just knowing where to find material of interest but also how to extrapolate the meaning of what they find. It is the analysis that is often the key.

Afterword

The purpose of this book has always been to help you help you and your clients feel safer.

That is my purpose in life; it is what has driven me most of my life and on reflection has been deeply embedded in me since I was a child.

What I hope you now understand is the terminology of security. Terms such as *risk*, *threat* and *vulnerability* are used daily. Knowing what these terms mean and how they interact is key to feeling safer, as you will now understand where they fit into your security plan and which elements you can influence to reduce the harm posed.

Many people become the subject of another's attention, and some of these people become fixated. Prominent people, be they famous, successful or known for other reasons, are more likely to be the subject of another's obsession. These obsessions are not homogenous. They are unique, and each one is motivated by different reasons and poses different levels of threats. What is known is that the recipient of such obsession very often becomes paranoid and hypervigilant. The cause of this is often the unknown element. Not knowing who the person of concern is, why they are fixated and whether they pose a threat are the causes of the fear. Understanding the motivating factors, the different grievances and the types of stalkers will help you make sense of these situations and resolve them, enabling you to retain control and identify the best strategy for tackling these issues and reduce the fear experienced by clients and the public.

Most people assume that when someone makes a threat, it is genuine, and their intention is to cause physical harm. You will know that that is not always the case, and rarely so. The issue of whether there is or has been an intimate relationship is a key factor in this, as well as the concept of affective or predatory violence. How a threat is communicated, by which channels, and how often can also be factors in its assessment. Social media plays a significant role in modern-day threats, with them being communicated freely via various platforms. You now know that most are designed to cause fear and intimidation rather than indicate any future violence.

Those individuals who *do* pose a threat rarely make it a direct threat. Those predators who stalk their prey will often indicate the threat they pose by one of eight proximal indicators, which, if unknown, will escape the most diligent researcher's attention as irrelevant. You, however, now know what these indicators are and will hopefully recognize them or seek further education to be even better informed. Equally, you will be alive to the power of your intuition and your in built threat assessment system, and the more you rely upon it, the better attuned you become to its power. Listen to your intuition and it will help you stay safe!

The workplace is increasingly becoming a place where threats, inappropriate behaviour and harassment are becoming the norm, and despite the presence of well-worded policies, the behaviours of concern are rarely recognized and reported, and those investigating continue to fail to understand the behavioural aspect of this issue. This is damaging brands' Environmental, Societal and Governance (ESG) credentials and causing great employees to leave, seek a better working environment; it also harms companies' reputations and financial status.

Event and function security, once the responsibility of law enforcement, is increasingly managed by private security professionals. Crowded places are attractive targets for terrorists and criminals, and private functions the target of the fixated superfan as well as the media seeking to exploit the privacy of this attending.

By now, you will be aware that being proactive is key and can prevent much of the intrusion and harm that is caused. Far too much private information is being leaked via the internet and the deep and dark web.

Some of that information is our own fault, unwittingly giving away too much and putting ourselves and our families at risk, while much of the data is stolen from global brands via cyber attacks and sold on the deep and dark web. A regular check-up will identify what private data is available and allow you to retake control of your safety.

The security industry has never had a hugely positive reputation, and despite government interventions, regulatory bodies being created, and legislation being enacted, the standards and quality are often disappointing. Despite that, some exceptional people working in our profession have dedicated their lives to keeping others safe. Many of these individuals have or are in the process of studying academically to support their operations skills, and some have gone a step further and become a Chartered Security Professional. I'd encourage you to do the same.

My hope is that this book has been enjoyable to read and educational.

Each chapter could have been a book, and, in some cases, further reading may prove advantageous. I have found the industry full of generous contributors keen to share their wisdom, and the very best are always the ones whose motivation, like mine, is to make a difference.

I hope this book has makes a difference for you.

Endnotes and further publications

Endnotes

[1] Fein, R.A. and Vossekuil, B. *Preventing Assassination: Secret Service Exceptional Case Study Project*. Washington, DC 1997 [cited 28 October 2018]. Available from: www.ncjrs.gov/pdffiles1/Photocopy/167224NCJRS.pdf

[2] Grindell, P. *The Defuse Podcast* [cited 27 May 2024]. Available from: https://defusepodcast.buzzsprout.com/1253126

[3] Definition of *security*. Cambridge Dictionary [cited 31 July 2024]. Available from: https://dictionary.cambridge.org/dictionary/english/security

[4] The *Guardian*. 'The Slow-burning Hatred That Led Thomas Mair to Murder Jo Cox' [cited 20 March 2023]. Available from: www.theguardian.com/uk-news/2016/nov/23/thomas-mair-slow-burning-hatred-led-to-jo-cox-murder

[5] Flynn, D., Moloney, E., Bhattarai, N., Scott, J., Breckons, M., Avery, L., et al. 'COVID-19 Pandemic in the United Kingdom'. *Health Policy Technology*, 1 December 2020, 9(4): 673 [cited 6 August 2024]. Available from: /pmc/articles/PMC7451057/

[6] Martin, P. *The Rules of Security*. Oxford University Press [cited 15 March 2023]. Available from: https://global.oup.com/academic/product/the-rules-of-security-9780198823575?cc=gb&lang=en&

[7] Research, Targeted Violence Research Team, Nebraska [cited 17 March 2023]. Available from: https://psychology.unl.edu/targeted-violence/research

[8] 'Kim Kardashian's Paris Robber Does Tell-All Interview About The Heist' [cited 18 March 2023]. Available from: www.buzzfeednews.com/article/stephaniesoteriou/kim-kardashian-paris-robber-guilt-details-interview

[9] London Evening Standard. '£5m Surrey Mansion Raided by Thieves' [cited 18 March 2023]. Available from: www.standard.co.uk/news/crime/

john-terry-s-ps5m-surrey-mansion-raided-by-thieves-after-he-posted-photo-of-skiing-holiday-on-instagram-a3598221.html

[10] Sky Sports (Boxing News). 'Amir Khan: Three Men Arrested After Boxer has £70,000 Watch Stolen at Gunpoint' [cited 18 March 2023]. Available from: www.skysports.com/boxing/news/12183/12638387/amir-khan-three-men-arrested-after-boxer-has-70-000-watch-stolen-at-gunpoint

[11] Dewan, A., Jordan, C., Halasz, S., George, S. 'London Mosque Attack Suspect Named, According to Media Outlets.' CNN [cited 18 March 2023]. Available from: www.cnn.com/2017/06/18/europe/urgent---london-vehicle-collision/index.html

[12] BBC News. London Nail Bombings Remembered 20 Years On [cited 18 March 2023]. Available from: www.bbc.co.uk/news/uk-england-london-47216594

[13] Brace, L. A Short Introduction to the Involuntary Celibate Sub-culture. Available from: www.crestresearch.ac.uk

[14] Mullen, P.E., James, D.V., Meloy, J.R., Pathé, M.T., Farnham, F.R., Preston, L., et al. 'The Fixated and the Pursuit of Public Figures.' *Journal of Forensic Psychiatry and Psychology*, 2009, 20(1): 33–47.

[15] Meloy, J.R. and Amman, M. 'Public Figure Attacks in the United States, 1995–2015.' *Behavioral Sciences and the Law*, 2016, September, 34(5): 622–644.

[16] James, D.V., Mullen, P.E., Meloy, J.R., Pathé, M.T., Preston, L., et al. 'Stalkers and Harassers of British Royalty: An Exploration of Proxy Behaviours for Violence.' *Behavioral Sciences and the Law*, 2010 [cited 23 October 2018]. Available from: www.interscience.wiley.com

[17] Washington Post. Text of Letter to Foster. Available from: www.washingtonpost.com/archive/politics/1981/04/02/text-of-letter-to-foster/eb0cfb7e-ffc2-47a3-90cf-c4f51b984775/

[18] Britannica. Islamic State in Iraq and the Levant (ISIL), History, Leadership, & Facts [cited 6 August 2024]. Available from: www.britannica.com/topic/Islamic-State-in-Iraq-and-the-Levant

[19] Britannica. Al-Qaeda, History, Meaning, Terrorist Attacks, & Facts [cited 6 August 2024]. Available from: www.britannica.com/topic/al-Qaeda

[20] Investopedia. Brexit Meaning and Impact: The Truth About the U.K. Leaving the EU [cited 6 August 2024]. Available from: www.investopedia.com/terms/b/brexit.asp

[21] BBC News. Thomas Mair: Extremist Loner Who Targeted Jo Cox [cited 6 August 2024]. Available from: www.bbc.co.uk/news/uk-38071894

22 Calhoun, F.S. and Weston, S.W. 'Rethinking the Path to Intended Violence' in *International Handbook of Threat Assessment*, April 2021 [cited March 22 2023, 392–406. Available from: https://academic.oup.com/book/30016/chapter/255632094

23 The Online Bodyguard® [cited 22 March 2023]. Available from: https://defusepodcast.buzzsprout.com/

24 Behavioral Threat Assessment Integration, Homeland Security [cited 6 August 2024]. Available from: www.dhs.gov/btai

25 Meloy, J.R. and Hoffmann, J. *International Handbook of Threat Assessment*, p. 736.

26 Suzy Lamplugh Trust [cited 6 August 2024]. Available from: www.suzylamplugh.org/

27 Crown Prosecution Service. Stalking [cited 15 May 2024]. Available from: www.cps.gov.uk/legal-guidance/stalking-or-harassment

28 What is Stalking and Harassment?, Police.UK [cited 31 July 2024]. Available from: www.police.uk/advice/advice-and-information/sh/stalking-harassment/what-is-stalking-harassment/

29 Mullen, P.E. 'Study of Stalkers.' *American Journal of Psychiatry*, 1999, August, 156(8): 1244–1249.

30 Super-Complaint on the Police Response to Stalking, GOV.UK [cited 6 August 2024]. Available from: www.gov.uk/government/publications/super-complaint-on-the-police-response-to-stalking

31 Dietz, E., Matthews, D.B., Martell, D., Stewart, T.M., Hrouda, D.R. and Warren. J. 'Threatening and Otherwise Inappropriate Letters to Members of the United States Congress.' *Journal of Forensic Sciences*, 1991, 36 [cited 15 November 2018]. Available from: https://s3.amazonaws.com/academia.edu.documents/39576862/Threatening_and_otherwise_inappropriate_20151031-15425-18lg6kh.pdf?AWSAccessKeyId=AKIAIWOWYYGZ2Y53UL3A&Expires=1542312808&Signature=%2BvjtvjvGQej2jhAmJnYqEDyx%2Ft8%3D&response-content-disposition=in

32 Meloy, J.R. 'Communicated Threats and Violence Toward Public and Private Targets: Discerning Differences Among Those Who Stalk and Attack.' *Journal of Forensic Sciences*, 2001, 46(5): 1211–1213 [cited 14 September 2018]. Available from: www.forensic.org

33 McEwan, T.E., Daffern, M, MacKenzie, R.D. and Ogloff, J.R.P. 'Risk Factors for Stalking Violence, Persistence, and Recurrence.' *Journal of Forensic Psychiatry and Psychology*, 2017, 28(1): 38–56.

34 Calhoun, F.S. and Weston. S.W. 'Imagining the Unimaginable to Prepare for the Unthinkable: Criteria for Detecting, Reporting, and Acting to Thwart Intended Violence.' *Journal of Threat Assessment and Management*, 27 February 2023. Available from: http://doi.apa.org/getdoi.cfm?doi=10.1037/tam0000200

35 Crown Prosecution Service. Hate Crime. Available from: www.cps.gov.uk/crime-info/hate-crime

36 The Investigation of Hate Crimes [cited 6 August 2024]. Available from: www.theiacp.org/resources/policy-center-resource/hate-crimes

37 BBC News. Labour MP Jo Cox 'Murdered for Political Cause' [cited 6 August 2024]. Available from: www.bbc.co.uk/news/uk-37978582

38 Harmange, P. *I Hate Men*. 2020. 4th Estate, 1–87.

39 Sky News. Sarah Everard Murder: How Killer Policeman Wayne Couzens Was Caught – and the Lengths He Went to Cover Up His Crime [cited 6 August 2024]. Available from: https://news.sky.com/story/sarah-everard-murder-how-killer-policeman-wayne-couzens-was-caught-and-the-lengths-he-went-to-cover-up-his-crime-12419714

40 The Guardian. David Carrick Jailed for Life Over Series of Rapes While Met Police Officer [cited 6 August 2024]. Available from: www.theguardian.com/society/2023/feb/07/david-carrick-jailed-life-rapes-met-police-officer

41 Ask For Angela [cited 6 August 2024]. Available from: https://askforangela.co.uk/

42 Glicken, M.D. and Robinson, B.C. *Treating Worker Dissatisfaction During Economic Change*, 2013. Academic Press.

43 L'Oréal Paris Stands Up Against Street Harassment [cited 31 July 2024]. Available from: www.loreal.com/en/articles/commitments/l-oreal-paris-stands-up-against-street-harassment/

44 Department for Digital CM and S. Rapid Evidence Assessment: The Prevalence and Impact of Online Trolling Department for Digital, Culture, Media and Sport [cited 29 March 2023]. Available from: chrome-extension://efaidnbmnnnibpcajpcglclefindmkaj/https://assets.publishing.service.gov.uk/government/uploads/system/uploads/attachment_data/file/973971/DCMS_REA_Online_trolling__V2.pdf

45 BBC News. The Saga of 'Pizzagate': The Fake Story That Shows How Conspiracy Theories Spread [cited 29 March 2023]. Available from: www.bbc.co.uk/news/blogs-trending-38156985

[46] ASIS International and SHRM Release American National Standard on Workplace Violence Prevention and Intervention [cited 30 March 2023]. Available from: www.ansi.org/news/standards-news/all-news/2011/10/asis-international-and-shrm-release-american-national-standard-on-workplace-violence-prevention-and-20

[47] Rugala, E.A. and Isaacs, Arnold R. (eds). Workplace Violence: Issues in Response Critical Incident Response Group National Center for the Analysis of Violent Crime FBI Academy, 2003 [cited 29 March 2023]. Available from: www.ojp.gov/ncjrs/virtual-library/abstracts/workplace-violence-issues-response

[48] Philpott, D. *The Workplace Violence Prevention Handbook* (2nd edn), 2019. Bernan Press, 1–251.

[49] Soerland, E. Van, Cutts, A., Szostak, T., Ma, Q. and Walsh, O. 'Better Safe Than Sorry: Identifying and Preventing Workplace Violence and Threats in Times of Economic Downturn' (white paper).

[50] TUC. Still Just a Bit of Banter? 2016 [cited 19 July 2023]. Available from: www.tuc.org.uk/research-analysis/reports/still-just-bit-banter

[51] Agency Central. Does The UK Have A Workplace Bullying Problem [cited 19 July 2023]. Available from: www.agencycentral.co.uk/articles/does-the-uk-have-a-workplace-bullying-problem/

[52] CIPD. Factsheet: Harassment And Bullying At Work, 2015 [cited 19 July 2023]. Available from: www.cipd.co.uk/hr-resources/factsheets/harassment-bullying-at-work.aspx

[53] Ontic [cited 6 August 2024]. Available from: https://ontic.co/

[54] Holbrook, C., Bixler, D, Rugala, E, and Casteel, C. *Workplace Violence Issues in Threat Management* (1st edn), 2020. Routledge, 11–112.

[55] Mundie, D.A., Perl, S. and Huth, C.L. 'Toward an Ontology for Insider Threat Research: Varieties of Insider Threat Definitions.' Workshop on Socio-Technical Aspects in Security and Trust, STAST, 2013, 26–36.

[56] Gelles, M. *Insider Threat: Prevention, Detection, Mitigation and Deterrence* (1st edn), 2016. Elsevier, 1–234.

[57] CPNI Insider Data Collection Study Report of Main Findings, 2013. Available from: www.cpni.gov.uk/advice/Personnel-security1/Online-social-networking

[58] Degrippo, S. 'Using the Present to Predict the Future.' *New Perimeters*, 2022 [cited 13 April 2023]. Available from: https://go.proofpoint.com/New-Perimeters-2022-Issue5.html#current-issue

59 Britannica. Edward Snowden [cited 6 August 2024]. Available from: www.britannica.com/biography/Edward-Snowden

60 BBC News. Lloyds Bank Worker Jessica Harper Jailed for £2.4m Fraud [cited 11 April 2023]. Available from: www.bbc.co.uk/news/uk-england-london-19675834

61 Bell, A.J.C., Rogers, M.B. and Pearce, J.M. 'The Insider Threat: Behavioral Indicators and Factors Influencing Likelihood of Intervention.' *International Journal of Critical Infrastructure Protection*, 2019, 1 March, 24: 166–176.

62 Cal/OSHA Workplace Violence Prevention for General Industry (Non-health Care Settings) [cited 6 August 2024]. Available from: www.dir.ca.gov/dosh/Workplace-Violence/General-Industry.html

63 Fein, R.A. and Vossekuil, B. 'Assassination in the United States: An Operational Study of Recent Assassins, Attackers, and Near-Lethal Approachers.' *Journal of Forensic Sciences*, 1999, March, 44(2): 14457J.

64 Calhoun, F.S. and Weston, S.W. *Threat Assessment and Management Strategies: Identifying the Howlers And Hunters*, 2016 (2nd edn) [cited 16 November 2018], 1–245. Available from: www.worldcat.org/title/threat-assessment-and-management-strategies-identifying-the-howlers-and-hunters/oclc/921240394?referer=di&ht=edition

65 Meloy, J. Reid and Hoffmann, J. *International Handbook of Threat Assessment*, 2014. Oxford University Press, 411 [cited 6 August 2018]. Available from: https://global.oup.com/academic/product/international-handbook-of-threat-assessment-9780199924554?cc=gb&lang=en&

66 The Guardian (Dodd, V. and Topping, A.) Roshonara Choudhry Jailed for Life Over MP Attack, 3 November 2010 [cited 6 December 2018]. Available from: www.theguardian.com/uk/2010/nov/03/roshonara-choudhry-jailed-life-attack

67 Pearson, E. 'The Case of Roshonara Choudhry: Implications for Theory on Online Radicalization, ISIS Women, and the Gendered Jihad.' *Policy Internet*, 2016, March, 8(1): 5–33.

68 The Guardian (Dodd, V.) Roshonara Choudhry: I Wanted to Die … I Wanted to Be a Martyr. 4 November 2010 [cited 3 April 2023]. Available from: https://www.theguardian.com/uk/2010/nov/04/stephen-timms-attack-roshonara-choudhry

69 Meloy, J.R., Habermeyer, E. and Guldimann, A. 'The Warning Behaviors of Anders Breivik.' *Journal of Threat Assessment and Management*, 2015, September–December, 2(3–4): 164–175.

70 WashingtonPost.com: Abortion Violence [cited 6 August 2024]. Available from: www.washingtonpost.com/wp-srv/national/longterm/abortviolence/stories/hill.htm

71 Calhoun, F.S. and Weston, S.W. *Threat Assessment and Management Strategies: Identifying The Howlers and Hunters* (2nd edn), 2016. (See note 65.)

72 Meloy, J.R. and O'Toole. M.E. 'The Concept of Leakage in Threat Assessment.' *Behavioral Sciences and the Law*, 2011, July, 29(4): 513–527 [cited 13 April 2023]. Available from: https://onlinelibrary.wiley.com/doi/full/10.1002/bsl.986

73 de Becker, G. *The Gift of Fear, Survival Signals That Protect Us From Violence*, 2000. Bloomsbury, 1–334.

74 Dylan Storm Roof's manifesto titled The Last Rhodesian, 2015 [cited 6 August 2024]. Available from: https://archive.org/details/the-last-rhodesian-by-dylan-storm-roof-2015

75 Relating to Dylan Storm Roof's manifesto: 'I Have No Choice'. CBS News [cited 12 April 2023]. Available from: www.cbsnews.com/news/dylann-roofs-manifesto-i-have-no-choice/

76 Reuters. Oath Keepers Leader Said Trump 'Will Need Us and Our Rifles', US Court Hears [cited 12 April 2023]. Available from: www.reuters.com/legal/government/oath-keepers-leader-said-trump-will-need-us-our-rifles-2022-10-04/

77 Meloy, J.R. and O'Toole. M.E. 'The Concept of Leakage in Threat Assessment.' *Behavioral Sciences and the Law*, 2011, July, 29(4): 513–527 [cited 13 April 2023]. Available from: https://onlinelibrary.wiley.com/doi/full/10.1002/bsl.986

78 Follman, M. *Trigger Points: Inside the Mission to Stop Mass Shootings in America*, 2022 (1st edn). New York: William Morrow, 1–286.

79 The Guardian. Alleged Neo-Nazi Admits Plotting Murder of MP Rosie Cooper, [cited 13 April 2023]. Available from: www.theguardian.com/uk-news/2018/jun/12/man-pleads-guilty-to-plot-to-labour-mp-rosie-cooper

80 Sky News. Timeline: Khalid Masood's Preparations for Westminster Attack [cited 12 April 2023]. Available from: https://news.sky.com/story/timeline-khalid-masoods-preparations-for-westminster-attack-11502510

81 BBC News. Liam Lyburd Mass Murder Plot: Teen Sentenced to Life [cited 6 August 2024]. Available from: www.bbc.co.uk/news/uk-england-tyne-34359392

[82] BBC News. Liam Lyburd Mass Murder Plot: Teen Sentenced to Life. (See note 82.)

[83] Meloy, J.R., Mohandie, K., Knoll, J.L. and Hoffmann, J. 'The Concept of Identification in Threat Assessment.' *Behavioral Sciences and the Law*, 2015, June, 33(2–3): 213–237.

[84] BBC News. Nail Bomber David Copeland Loses Sentence Appeal [cited 6 August 2024]. Available from: www.bbc.co.uk/news/uk-england-london-13946298

[85] Newsweek, J.D. Salinger's Influence [cited 14 April 2023]. Available from: www.newsweek.com/jd-salingers-influence-70857

[86] Izak, K. Anders Behring Breivik. 'A Case Study of a Far-Right Terrorist – A Lone Wolf (Part I).' *Terroryzm*, 2022, September, (2): 280–314.

[87] Poppe, K. Nidal Hasan – A Case Study in Lone-Actor Terrorism, 2018. PDF available at: https://extremism.gwu.edu/sites/g/files/zaxdzs5746/files/Nidal%20Hasan.pdf

[88] National Threat Assessment Centre. Using a Systems Approach for Threat Assessment Investigations: A Case Study on Jared Lee Loughner, 2015 [cited 31 August 2018]. Available from: www.secretservice.gov/data/protection/ntac/Jared_Loughner_Using_Systems.pdf

[89] Murderpedia. Jared Loughner [cited 6 August 2024]. Available from: https://murderpedia.org/male.L/l/loughner-jared.htm

[90] College of Policing. Counter Terrorism Security Coordinator (CT SecCo) [cited 17 August 2024]. Available from: www.college.police.uk/career-learning/courses/counter-terrorism-security-coordinator-ct-secco

[91] NPSA. Hostile Vehicle Mitigation (HVM) [cited 17 August 2024]. Available from: www.npsa.gov.uk/hostile-vehicle-mitigation-hvm

[92] PBS News. New Details Emerge on Vienna Terror Plots Behind Taylor Swift Concert Cancellations [cited 17 August 2024]. Available from: www.pbs.org/newshour/show/new-details-emerge-on-vienna-terror-plots-behind-taylor-swift-concert-cancellations

[93] Hughes, Kieran. *Terror Attack Brighton: Blowing Up the Iron Lady*. 2015, Pen & Sword Books, 159.

[94] FBI. Update on the FBI Investigation of the Attempted Assassination of Former President Donald Trump [cited 17 August 2024]. Available from: www.fbi.gov/news/press-releases/update-on-the-fbi-investigation-of-the-attempted-assassination-of-former-president-donald-trump

95 New York Times (Whitney, C.R.) IRA Attacks 10 Downing Street with Mortar Fire as Cabinet Meets, 8 February 1991 [cited 17 August 2024]. Available from: www.nytimes.com/1991/02/08/world/ira-attacks-10-downing-street-with-mortar-fire-as-cabinet-meets.html

96 Henriques, R. The Independent Review of the Metropolitan Police Service's Handling of Non-Recent Sexual Offence Investigations Alleged Against Persons of Public Prominence [cited 17 August 2024]. Available from: www.met.police.uk/police-forces/metropolitan-police/areas/about-us/about-the-met/henriques-report/

97 Schilling, Dan. *The Power of Awareness: And Other Secrets from the World's Foremost Spies, Detectives, and Special Operators on How to Stay Safe and Save Your Life*, 2021 [cited 30 May 2024]. Grand Central Publishing. Available from: www.barnesandnoble.com/w/the-power-of-awareness-dan-schilling/1137837298

98 London Evening Standard. John Terry's £5m Surrey Mansion Ransacked by Thieves While Chelsea Star 'Was Away on Skiing Holiday' [cited 24 April 2023]. Available from: www.standard.co.uk/news/crime/john-terry-s-ps5m-surrey-mansion-ranksacked-by-thieves-while-chelsea-star-was-away-on-skiing-holiday-a3481541.html

99 de Becker, G. *The Gift of Fear, Survival Signals That Protect Us From Violence*, 2000. Bloomsbury.

100 Wong, P. Intuition: The Best Kept Secret for Survival and Success [cited 21 April 2023]. Available from: www.drpaulwong.com/intuition-the-best-kept-secret-for-survival-and-success/

101 Chilling Crimes. Clare Bernal [cited 6 August 2024]. Available from: www.chillingcrimes.com/blogs/news/clare-bernal

102 Office of National Statistics. Perceptions of Personal Safety and Experiences of Harassment, Great Britain 16 February to 13 March 2022 [cited 20 April 2023]. Available from: www.ons.gov.uk/peoplepopulation andcommunity/crimeandjustice/bulletins/perceptionsofpersonalsafety andexperiencesofharassmentgreatbritain/16februaryto13march2022#:~:text =The%20latest%20Opinions%20and%20Lifestyle,from%2058%25%20in%20 June%202021

103 New York Post (Kesslen, B.) Kim Kardashian Robber Blames Star For Infamous Paris Hotel Heist, 21 August 2022. Available at: https://nypost. com/2022/08/21/kim-kardashian-robber-feels-no-remorse-blames-star-for-the-heist/

[104] Aviation Safety. What Is Proactive Risk Management in Aviation SMS? [cited 17 May 2023]. Available from: https://aviationsafetyblog.asms-pro.com/blog/what-is-proactive-risk-management-in-aviation-sms-programs

[105] BBC on This Day. 1984: Memories of the Brighton Bomb [cited 31 March 2023]. Available from: http://news.bbc.co.uk/onthisday/hi/witness/october/12/newsid_3665000/3665388.stm

[106] The Ponemon Institute. Cost of Insider Threats Global Report, 2022. (See also www.intrasource.co.uk/blog/it-security/cost-of-insider-threats/)

[107] See www.gov.uk/government/organisations/security-industry-authority/about#responsibilities

[108] Statista. UK Security Industry Workforce, 2023 [cited 1 June 2024]. Available from: www.statista.com/statistics/780333/security-industry-employees-uk/

Further publications

International Handbook of Threat Assessment (2nd edn) (Oxford University Press, 2021).

Preventing Assassination: Secret Service Exceptional Case Study Project (National Institute of Justice, 1997).

The Gift of Fear: Survival Signals That Protect Us from Violence (Bloomsbury, 2000).

The Power of Awareness, and Other Secrets from the World's Foremost Spies, Detectives, and Special Operators on How to Stay Safe and Save Your Life (Grand Central Publishing, 2021).

The Rules of Security: Staying Safe in a Risky World (Oxford University Press, 2019).

The Workplace Violence Prevention Handbook (Rowman & Littlefield, 2019).

Threat Assessment and Management Strategies (Routledge, 2016).

Trigger Points, Inside the Mission to Stop Mass Shootings in America (Dey Street Books, 2022).

Acknowledgements

I have always loved books and yet the thought of writing one of my own is an intimidating experience. To do so requires discipline and the ability to park one's imposter syndrome. Without my wife Amanda's belief in me, this book would have been impossible to write.

My first draft was clumsy and a poor reflection of what I hope this book now is, and for that I must thank my publisher Alison Jones from Practical Inspiration Publishing who demonstrated extraordinary patience in helping me to accomplish my goal of becoming an author.

The genesis of the knowledge behind this book was formed from the tragedy of the assassination of Jo Cox MP and the faith that Neil Basu, at that time the Assistant Commissioner for Specialist Operations in the [UK] Metropolitan Police and the National Police Chiefs' Council lead for Counter Terrorism Policing had in me to make a difference. I hope I didn't let him down.

I was especially fortunate to have been introduced to the subject of targeted violence and communicated threats by Dr Robert Fein and to Dr Reid Meloy, and Dr Frederick S. Calhoun who have been mentors and a constant source of inspiration and guidance.

My journey would have been impossible without the support and patience of Alison Young, George Allan, Paul Williams and Vincent McMillan, the original members of the Metropolitan Police Parliamentary Liaison and Investigation Team (PLaIT), and to Simon Causer, Audrey Shannon and Jane Johnson QPM, who had to manage my frustrations and guide my enthusiasm in equal measures.

I am eternally grateful for the wisdom and generosity of all those who have shared their knowledge on The Defuse Podcast, and to my friends and colleagues from the Association of Threat Assessment Professionals and the Association of European Threat Assessment Professionals.

The following were early readers who offered suggestions for improvement: Bryan Flannery, Melissa Muir, Andrew Donaldson and Dr Lorraine Sheridan.

The author

As the CEO and founder of Defuse Global, a consultancy specializing in threat investigation and crisis management, Philip Grindell is a recognized specialist in identifying, assessing and managing threats and toxic behaviour for prominent individuals, private clients and organizations.

With almost 30 years of experience as a Scotland Yard Detective, including a three-year secondment to British Intelligence, Philip honed his skills in threat intelligence, risk management and protective security.

Philip served as a Counter-Terrorism Security Coordinator, securing high-profile events, involving members of the UK Royal Family and Government ministers, preparing detailed contingency plans preventing terrorist and other attacks.

His expertise in identifying physical, reputational and psychological threats was put to the test during his time setting up and was instrumental in putting together the Parliamentary Liaison and Investigation Team (PLaIT), a new protective intelligence and workplace violence team in the UK Parliament following the assassination of Jo Cox MP in 2016.

Having been taught threat assessment directly by Dr Robert Fein, one of the authors of the US Secret Service's Exceptional Case Study Project, Philip has unparalleled expertise in the field of behavioural threat assessment and management.

Philip successfully identified the threat that prevented the next attack on a Member of Parliament and a serving police officer.

With an MSc in Security Management, and as a Chartered Security professional, Philip has become one of the UK's most trusted leaders and advisors in lone actor, fixated and workplace threats.

Philip launched The Defuse Podcast in 2022, bringing together globally renowned experts to discuss the latest research and practices that ensure the safety of family offices and HNW individuals, and produces a weekly newsletter, Defuse News®, every Monday.

www.defuseglobal.com/resources/

www.linkedin.com/in/behavioural-threat-management-specialist/

Index

4Chan 53
7/7 London bombings 24, 80, 85
9/11 attacks 80

A
Abbas, Yunis 141–142
abortion services
  anti-abortionists 22
  attacks on 72
accept (RARA risk assessment model)
    12, 13
accidents 11
acquisitive crime 17
activists
  events and functions security 98, 103
  pathway to violence 69
Admiral Duncan bar, Soho, London 17
AETAP (Association of European
    Threat Assessment Individuals)
    156
AfATAP (Africa) 156
agency staff 100
'agent handling' training 121
airborne attacks, events and functions
    security 98, 104–105, 107
airspace restrictions 104
airspace restrictions, UK 104
ALATAP (Latin America) 156
alcohol consumption 51, 135, 137
Alefantis, James 52–53
Al-Qaeda 22, 99
Amman, M. 20
analyse risk, SAFER Model® process 160
Anderson, Ailsa 142
anger, and grievances 24, 25
animal rights groups 22
anonymity 40, 144–145
anti-immigration sentiment 5
APATAP (Asia-Pacific) 156
Ariane Grande concert attack,
    Manchester 2017 85–86

ASIS 156
'Ask for Angela' scheme 49
ATAP (US) 156
attack stage, in the pathway to violence
    73
auditory senses 116
autistic spectrum 91
autonomic arousal 15, 16
aviation safety 151
avoid (RARA risk assessment model)
    12, 13

B
bag searches 97, 101
Bardo, Robert 87
Becker, Gavin de 128–129
Beech, Carl 112–113
behaviour
  behavioural indicators of threat
      escalation 74–75
  behavioural threat analysis 26
  behavioural threat management 44
  pre-attack warning behaviours 77–94
Bernal, Clare 130
Bhaker, Suky 48
bias 112–113
biological attacks 98, 101–102
blame, and grievances 24, 25
body language 115, 123
Breivik, Anders Behring 72 , 88, 91
Brexit 23, 40, 52
Brexit, and Parliamentary security 4–5
bullying, workplace violence 57, 59–60

C
Calhoun, F.S. 24, 41–42, 45, 46, 70–73
Canadian Parliament attack, 2014 91
capability 8, 9, 10
Capitol building, Washington, 6 January
    2021 attack 80
car-ramming *see* vehicle-based attack

CATAP (Canada) 156
Catcher in the Rye 87
causes, and fixated people 22–23
CCTV 134
'cease and desist' letter 30
CEOs
   fraud by 65
   workplace violence 57, 58–59
Chapman, Mark 26, 86–87
Chartered Security Professionals 167
chemical attacks 98, 101–102
child sex abuse 82
   Operation Midland 112–113
Choudhry, Roshonara 71, 72
Cirillo, Nathan 91
clients, workplace violence 56
Clinton, Hillary 52–53
close protection teams 97
closed questions 114–115
Columbine school attack 80
Comet Ping Pong 52–53
commentary, while driving 122–123
communicated threats 39–41, 43–45,
      53–54, 78
   hate crime 47–50
   Hunters and Howlers 41–43, 44,
      53–54, 76, 81
   intimacy factor 41
   physical, reputational and
      psychological harm 50–53
   reporting criteria 46–47
communication
   last resort behaviours 78–79
   multiple sources of 74
   sudden cessation of 75
communication plan, events and
      functions security 99
complacency, danger of 149–154
confidentiality, insider threats 65
confirmation bias 112
conflict avoidance, and personal safety
      135, 137
conflict resolution training 133
Cooper, Rosie 82, 85
Copeland, David 17, 86
copying, of previous attackers 85, 86–88

counterfeit merchandise 105
counter-reconnaissance teams 97
'course of conduct' 29, 38, 75
COVID-19 pandemic 7
Cox, Jo 5, 16, 22–23, 48, 152
crime prevention and detection, events
      and functions security 98
criminal acts
   events and functions security 98,
      105–106
   and personal safety 135, 137
   social media information 121–122
   street robberies 123–124
criminal damage, reporting of 46
criminal intent, in workplace violence
      56
'crossing the line' 70
crowd control 97
Crown Prosecution Service 30–31
C-suite executives 57–59
CT SecCo (Counter Terrorist Security
      Coordinators) 95, 102–103, 107
C-UAS (counter-unmanned aerial
      system) technologies 104–105
culture 160–161
customers, workplace violence 56
cyber attacks 104, 107, 167
cyber security 97, 143–144
   see also privacy
cyber stalking 32
cycle robberies 123–124

D
data brokers 143–144
dates
   specific reference to as threat indicator
      75
   as triggering events 80–81
death 46
death threats, towards women 48–49
decision-making, impact of
      psychological attacks on 51–52
Defuse Global 36, 68, 164
Defuse Podcast 36, 41, 48, 113–114, 127
delusional beliefs 46, 74–75
depression 51

'Detect, Report, Act' pre-identification
      phase 45
diary-keeping stalking 35
disabled people
   disability hate crime 47
   personal safety 134
disciplinary outcomes, reporting of 46
distance attacks, events and functions
      security 98, 102–103
diversity, in the security profession 156
Domestic Counter Terrorism Unit 82
domestic violence, and stalking 33, 41
Downing Street mortar attacks
      102–103
Dresden, Germany 104
driving, commentary and situational
      awareness 122–123
drone attacks, events and functions
      security 98, 104–105, 107
drug dealing 105
drug use, and personal safety 135, 137
drug-related behaviour 75
due diligence 63–64, 100, 153

E
economic decline, and increase in
      threats and violence 39, 49,
      56–57
Emanuel Methodist Church,
      Charleston, South Carolina 79
emergency numbers 137
Emerson, Ralph Waldo 128
emotions
   escalation of 75
   and physical violence 15, 16, 69
employment and employees
   agency staff 100
   pre-employment vetting 63–64
   in the security profession 158
   workplace violence 56
employment tribunals 60
end-of-life behaviours 72
   Khalid Masood 83
energy burst 78, 91–92
engage and liaise, SAFER Model®
      process 161–162

environmentalists 22
Equality Act 2010 59
erratic behaviour 75
escalation see threat escalation
ESG (Environmental, Societal and
      Governance) credentials 166
ETDs (explosive trace detectors) 102
evacuation plans 98–99
events and functions security 95–98,
      106–108, 166
   activists/protestors 98, 103
   airborne/UAV/drone attacks 98,
      104–105, 107
   attack methodologies 98
   criminal acts 98, 105–106
   distance/sniper attack 98, 102–103
   human/lone actor threat 98, 101
   IED (improvized explosive devices)
      attacks 98, 101–102
   insider threat 98, 100
   invacuation or evacuation? 98–99
   technical attacks 98, 104, 107
   vehicle-based attack 98, 99–100
Everard, Sarah 6, 49
extremist activity 16
   right-wing groups 5, 22–23, 89
   social media 144–145
   targeted attacks by 18

F
Family Liaison service 163–164
FBI 56, 77
   Behavioural Science Unit 82
fight-or-flight response 127, 130
'final acts' 46, 72
   Khalid Masood 83
financial gain, insider threats 63, 64
Finsbury Park Mosque, London 17
Fixated Threat Assessment Centre,
      London 20
fixated threats 19, 165
   fixated people 19–23, 44, 96–97
   grievances 23–27
flags 88
forensic assessment, SAFER Model®
      process 160–161

Fort Hood, US, military base attack 2009 89–90
Foster, Jodie 21–22, 87
FOUR (Fixated, Obsessive, Unwanted, Repeated) 31
fraud, insider threats 65
functions *see* events and functions security

G
gaming 91
Gifford, Gabby 92
grievances 23–27
    case study 26–27
    desire for notoriety 25–26
    stage in the pathway to violence 70, 71, 73
    workplace violence 58
'gut instinct' 128, 131
    see also intuition

H
hackers 143–144
harassment 34, 43, 75, 130, 134
    social media 146
    of women in public spaces 50
    workplace violence 57, 59–60
    see also sexual harassment
'Harassment Bystander Training,' Suzy Lamplugh Trust 50
Harmange, Pauline 48–49
Harper, Jessica 64
Hasan, Nidal 89–90
hate crime 47–50
    Dylan Roof 79
Health and Safety Act 67
Health and Safety Executive 11
Hett, Martyn 85–86, 107
high-net-worth venues, targeted attacks 17
Hill, Paul 72
Hinkley, John Jr. 21–22, 87
HMICFRS (His Majesty's Inspectorate of Constabulary and Fire and Rescue Services) 34

HMV (hostile vehicle mitigation) systems 99–100
home security 2, 36
homejacking 140–144
homicides 33, 34, 38, 49
    homicidal ideation 74, 79
'horizon scanning' 122–123
hotels, and personal safety 135, 137
Howlers 41–43, 44, 53–54, 76, 81
humiliation, and grievances 24, 25
Hunters and Howlers 41–43, 44, 53–54, 76, 81
'hunting' phase of planned attack 16
hypervigilance 4, 37, 51, 109, 163, 165

I
identification
    identification phase, threat assessments 45–46
    pre-attack warning behaviour 78, 85–90
identify risk, SAFER Model® process 160
identity theft 65
ideology
    fixated people 22–23
    insider threats 63
IED (improvized explosive device) attacks 98, 101–102
inappropriate behaviour, reporting of 46
incels, targeted attacks by 18
Incompetent Suitor (stalker type) 33
in-house security 97
injustice 46
inner voice 128
    see also intuition
insider threats 39, 62–66
    events and functions security 98, 100
insignia 88
instinct 127–128
intended attacks *see* targeted/intended attacks
intent 8, 9, 10
internet 29, 32, 39, 44

see also online security and privacy; social media

interrogation 111

intervention 81

in public harassment 50

interviewing 111–112, 117

bias 112–113

body language 115, 123

multi-sensory approach 115–117

planning and strategy 114, 117

question types 114–115, 117

rapport 113–114, 117

intimacy factor, communicated threats 41, 43, 54

Intimacy Seeker (stalker type) 33

intimate relationships 21, 27, 33, 43, 54, 76, 165

intrusive behaviour 2

intuition 128–131, 136

invacuation 99

investigations, workplace violence 66–67

IPSOS 50

IRA (Irish Republican Army) 102–103, 152, 154

ISIS 22, 89, 99

Islamic extremism 22, 24, 71, 83, 89–90

K

Kardashian, Kim 17, 140–144, 147

Khan, Amir 17

Khan, Mohammed Sidique 24

kinaesthetic people 116

knife crime 134

L

last resort behaviours 78–80

leakage, pre-attack warning behaviour 78, 81–84, 85

legal representatives, in interviews 113

Lennon, John 26, 86–87

LGBTQ+-based venues, targeted attacks 17

LinkedIn 65

listening skills 112, 114

location, specific reference to as threat indicator 75

lone actors 22, 27, 44, 89

events and functions security 98, 101

pathway to violence 69

L'Oréal Paris 50

loss 24, 25, 46

Loughner, Jared Lee 92

'low risk' 15

loyalty to friends/family/country 63

Lymburd, Liam 83–84

M

Mair, Thomas 5, 23

manifestos 72, 85, 89

Dylan Roof 79

marginalized groups, targeted attacks by 18

Martin, Paul 9

Martyn's Law 96, 107

Masood, Khalid 83

McVeigh, Timothy 88

'Me too' movement 48

media strategy 140

Meer, Bram B. van der 113–114

Meloy, Reid 20, 25, 40–41

men

misogyny 47–50

personal safety 134

mental health 163

see also psychological attacks

mental illness 20, 31, 70

Merkel, Angela 104

misogyny 47–50

moped robberies 123–124

Morris, Desmond 115

motivation, pre-attack warning behaviour 84–85

MPs (Members of Parliament) *see* Parliamentary security

MSc in Security Management 43–44

Muir, Melissa 63–64

Mullen, P.E. 33–34

multi-discipline teams, workplace violence 67

multi-sensory approach in interviewing
115–117
murder *see* homicides
Murray, Figen 85–86

N
narcissistic personality disorder 59
National Action 82
National Stalking Consortium 34
national threat level 8–9
Navarro, Joe 115
Nazi ideologies 5, 82, 89
NDM (National Decision-making
Model) 13–15
no-fly zones 104
Northern Ireland 6, 151–152
notoriety, desire for 25–26
novel aggression, pre-attack warning
behaviour 78, 90–91, 93
NPSA (National Protective Security
Authority) 62–63, 64

O
Office of National Statistics, Perceptions
of Personal Safety and
Experiences of Harassment
report 134
online security and privacy 36, 139–147,
150, 151, 152–153
Ontic Centre for Protective Intelligence
57
open questions 114–115
Operation Midland 112–113
organizations, reporting criteria 46–47
Osborne, Darren 17
OSINT (Open Source Intelligence) 103
oversharing, risks of 142
Oxford University 39, 56–57

P
Palmer, Keith 83
paranoia 4, 11, 29, 37, 46, 51, 75, 109,
163, 165
parking control, events and functions
security 97
Parliamentary security 4–5, 12, 152

abuse towards politicians 40
attacks on 44
'Howler' threat to politicians 43–44
misogyny towards female politicians
48
physical harm, threats of 50–51
pre-attack warning behaviours 82–83
psychological attacks 52
social media 40, 74
pathological fixation 20, 22, 78
see also fixated threats
'Pathway to Intended or Targeted
Violence, The' (US Secret
Service) 69–70
Pathway to Intended Violence, The
(Calhoun and Weston) 70–73
Pech, Michael 130
performance, impact of psychological
attacks on 51–52
personal biases (prejudices) 112
personal information, sale of 143–144
personal responsibility 149
see also complacency, danger of
personal safety 133–137
personal workplace violence 56
personality disorders, pathway to
violence 70
physical effects of psychological attacks
51–52
physical senses 116
physical violence
affective or impulsive 15
predatory or targeted 15, 16
threats of 46, 50–51
planning 46
Podesta, John 52–53
police and policing
NDM (National Decision-making
Model) 13–15
personal safety training 133–134
stalking 34, 37–38
threat reporting 46
women's lack of trust in 0, 6, 49
politicians *see* Parliamentary security
pre-attack warning behaviours 77–78, 94
copying of previous attackers 85, 86–88

energy burst 78, 91–92
identification 78, 85–90
last resort behaviours 78–80
leakage 78, 81–84, 85
motivation 84–85
novel aggression 78, 90–91, 93
triggering events 80–81
Predatory Stalker (stalker type) 34
predictability 140
predictable behaviour 17
pre-employment vetting 63–64
prejudices (personal biases) 112
preparation/pre-attack stage in the
pathway to violence 71–72
privacy 139, 166–167
and public relations 139–144
proactivity 149–154, 166
proactive due diligence 63–64
probing and breach stage in the pathway
to violence 72–73
problematic people 44, 45, 58, 73
problematic terminations, reporting of 46
protestors, events and functions security
98, 103
proximal warning behaviours see pre-
attack warning behaviours
proximity
event and function security 96–97
fixated persons' desire for 21, 27
pseudo commando 85
Anders Behring Breivik 88
pseudonyms 122
psychological attacks 16, 39, 50–52
public relations (PR), and privacy
139–144
public spaces, targeted attacks 18
public transport, unwanted behaviour
on 48

Q
questions, in interviewing 114–115

R
race hate crime 47
targeted attacks on race-based venues 17
radiological attacks 98, 101–102

rape, victim interviewing 116–117
rapport, in interviews 113–114, 117
RARA (reduce, accept, remove, avoid)
risk assessment model 12–13
Reagan, Ronald 21–22, 87
recognition, desire for 63
reduce (RARA risk assessment model)
12, 13
Rejected Stalker (stalker type) 33
religious hate crime 47
targeted attacks on religion-based
venues 17
remove (RARA risk assessment model)
12, 13
Renshaw, Jack 82
reporting 46
communicated threats 46–47
insider threats 65
social media threats 146
reputational attacks 16, 50
research and planning stage in the
pathway to violence 71
Resentful Stalker (stalker type) 33
revenge, desire for 46, 63
reviews, importance of 153–154
Rhodes, Stephen 80
risk 7–8, 18, 165
'low risk' 15
'unknown risk' 15
risk assessment 7, 8
analyse risk, SAFER Model® process
160
stalking 32
risk management 10–11
risk management and reassure, SAFER
Model® process 162–164
risk matrix 11
risk register 11
'risk tolerance' 8
Roof, Dylan 79
Royal Family (UK) 20, 95, 96, 97,
105–106, 140, 142

S
SAFER Model® process 158–164
safety 1–2, 6, 18

Schaeffer, Rebecca 87
Schilling, Dan 120, 124, 127
schools 45
  school shooters, pathway to violence 69
  targeted attacks 18
scooter robberies 123–124
searches, physical 103
security 1–2, 6, 18
Security Industry Authority 155
security profession 155–158, 167
security risk management 10–11
security systems, testing of 46
self-discipline 154
serial killers 82, 129
sexual assault 16, 34, 105
sexual harassment
  workplace violence 57, 60–61
  see also harassment
sexual orientation hate crime 47
  targeted attacks on venues 17
shopping centres 18, 45
situational awareness 119–125, 136, 150
sniper attacks 96, 98, 102–103
Snowdon, Edward 64
social media 39, 44, 53, 166
  action if threatened on 145–146
  Parliamentary security 40, 52
  risks of 140–146
  'screening' of 73–74
  and situational awareness 121–122
  stalking and harassment 29, 30, 31, 32
South America 157
SPOC (single point of contact) 98, 107
stalking 2, 16, 26–27, 29, 30–32, 38, 48,
    75, 165, 166
  action if clients are being stalked 35–36
  dealing with victims of 36–38
  domestic stalkers 41
  event and function security 96–97
  online assessment website 34
  pathway to violence 69
  risk factors 34–35
  security measures 36
  social media 146
  stalking advocates 36, 37–38
  types of behaviour 31–32

types of stalkers 33–34
stewards 97
strategy phase, SAFER Model® process
  159–160
street robberies 123–124
Structure Professional Judgement (SPJ)
  tools 160
'Study of Stalkers' (Mullen) 33–34
suicide
  psychological attacks 51
  suicidal ideation 46, 74, 79
suicide attacks 99
'superfans' 96–97
surveillance 46, 121
  CCTV 134
Suzy Lamplugh Trust 30, 34, 36, 48, 50

T
targeted/intended attacks 15–18, 27, 44
  general crime 17
  and grievances 26
  pathway to 69–73, 76, 78
  planning of 16–17
Taylor Swift concert, Austria, 2024 100
technical attacks, events and functions
  security 98, 104, 107
terrorism
  'manifestos' of terrorists 24
  pathway to violence 69
  targeted/intended attacks 16
  UK's national threat level 8–9
  workplace violence 56
Terry, John 17, 122
Thatcher, Margaret 102, 152
threat 1–2, 7, 8–9, 18, 165
threat assessments 9, 43–44
  communicated threats 39–40
  'Detect, Report, Act' pre-identification
    phase 45
  event security plans 96–97
  identification phase 45–46
  reporting criteria 46
threat escalation 69, 76
  behavioural indicators 74–75
  identification of 73–76
  pathway to violence 69–73, 76

threat management 10–11, 76
  behavioural threat management 44
threatening behaviours 16
ticket touts 105
'ticking time bombs' 58
time, specific reference to as threat
        indicator 75
Timms, Stephen 71
Trade Union Congress 57
transgender identity 47
triggering events 80–81
trolls 42, 52
Trump, Donald 80, 102, 107
trust
  women's lack of trust in police 6, 49, 134
  in workplace violence investigations
        66, 68
Tucson killing spree, 2011 92

U
UAV attacks, events and functions
        security 98, 104–105, 107
unconscious bias 112
uniforms 88
University of Nebraska Targeted
        Violence research team 16
'unknown risk' 15
unwanted attention 29, 38, 165
  'course of conduct' requirement 29, 38
  harassment 29–30, 34, 38
  stalking 29, 30–38
US Secret Service 77, 107
  Exceptional Case Study Report 40–41
  'Pathway to Intended or Targeted
        Violence, The' 69–70

V
vehicles
  events and functions security 97, 98,
        99–100
  and personal safety 136, 137, 154
venues
  search teams 97
  targeted attacks 17
  see also events and functions security
verification bias 112

vetting 63–64, 153
victims
  intuition 128–129, 131
  see also interviewing
violence
  reporting of 46
  specific reference to as threat indicator
        76
  violent ideation stage in the pathway
        70–71
visual senses 116
vulnerability 7, 9–10, 18, 165
  and situational awareness 119–120

W
war games 88, 91
warrior mentality 85
weapons 46
  acquisition of 71, 72
  specific reference to as threat indicator
        76
West, Kanye 141
Weston, S.W. 24, 41–42, 45, 46, 70–73
whaling 65
white suprematists 5, 22–23, 79, 82
women
  death threats 48–49
  lack of trust in police 6, 49, 134
  misogyny 47–50
  personal safety 134
  and stalking 31
  threats in public spaces 50
  workplace violence 57
Worker Protection (Amendment of
        Equality Act 2010) Act 2023 60, 67
workplace violence 39, 45, 55–56,
        58–59, 67–68, 166
  bullying and harassment 59–60
  causes 56–58
  insider threats 62–66
  investigations 66–67
  sexual harassment 60–61, 130
  targeted attacks 18

Z
Zehaf-Bibeau, Michael 91

A quick word from Practical Inspiration Publishing...

We hope you found this book both practical and inspiring – that's what we aim for with every book we publish.

We publish titles on topics ranging from leadership, entrepreneurship, HR and marketing to self-development and wellbeing.

Find details of all our books at: www.practicalinspiration.com

 Did you know...

We can offer discounts on bulk sales of all our titles – ideal if you want to use them for training purposes, corporate giveaways or simply because you feel these ideas deserve to be shared with your network.

We can even produce bespoke versions of our books, for example with your organization's logo and/or a tailored foreword.

To discuss further, contact us on info@practicalinspiration.com.

 Got an idea for a business book?

We may be able to help. Find out more about publishing in partnership with us at: bit.ly/PIpublishing.

Follow us on social media...

🐦 @PIPTalking

📷 @pip_talking

🅕 @practicalinspiration

♪ @piptalking

🅛 Practical Inspiration Publishing